my **revision** notes

AS Edexcel History
HENRY VIII: AUTHORITY, NATION AND RELIGION 1509–40

Peter Clements

Series editors:
Robin Bunce and
Laura Gallagher

HODDER
EDUCATION
AN HACHETTE UK COMPANY

Acknowledgements

The Publishers would like to thank the following for permission to produce copyright material:

Anthony Fletcher: extract from *Tudor Rebellions* (Longman, 1968); **Nancy Lenz Harvey**: extracts from *Thomas, Cardinal Wolsey* (Macmillan, 1981), copyright © 1980 by Nancy Lenz Harvey. All rights reserved. Reprinted by permission of Scribner, a Division of Simon & Schuster, Inc; **Robert Hutchinson**: extracts from *Thomas Cromwell* (Weidenfeld & Nicolson, 2007); **E. W. Ives**: extract from 'Will the Real Henry VIII Please Stand Up?' from *History Today*, 56/2 (2006); extract from 'The Fall of Wolsey' from *Cardinal Wolsey, Church, State & Art*, edited by S.J.Gunn and P.G. Lindley (Cambridge University Press, 1991); **Geoffrey Moorhouse**: extract from *The Pilgrimage of Grace* (Weidenfeld & Nicolson, 2002); **J. R. H. Moorman**: extracts from *A History of the Church of England*, Third edition (Morehouse-Barlow, 1973); **M. D. Palmer**: extracts from *Henry VIII*, Second edition (Longman, 1984), reprinted by permission of Pearson Education; **David H. Pill**: extract from *The English Reformation, 1529–58* (Hodder & Stoughton, 1973); **Keith Randell**: extracts from *Henry VIII and the Reformation in England* (Access to History), Second/revised edition (Hodder Education, 2001), reprinted by the permission of the Publisher; **Josephine Ross**: extracts from *The Tudors* (Artus Publishing 1979; Orion, 1995), © Josephine Ross, reprinted by permission of the author and Aitken Alexander Associates; **J. J. Scarisbrick**: extracts from *Henry VIII* (Methuen, 1968); **David Starkey**: extracts from 'Privy Secrets: Henry VIII and the Lords of the Council' from *History Today*, Volume 37, Issue 8 (August, 1987); **Giles Tremlett**: extracts from *Catherine of Aragon* (Faber & Faber, 2010); **Derek Wilson**: extracts from *A Brief History of Henry VIII* (Robinson, 2009), reproduced by permission of Constable & Robinson.

Every effort has been made to trace all copyright holders, but if any have been inadvertently overlooked the Publishers will be pleased to make the necessary arrangements at the first opportunity.

Although every effort has been made to ensure that website addresses are correct at time of going to press, Hodder Education cannot be held responsible for the content of any website mentioned in this book. It is sometimes possible to find a relocated web page by typing in the address of the home page for a website in the URL window of your browser.

Hachette UK's policy is to use papers that are natural, renewable and recyclable products and made from wood grown in sustainable forests. The logging and manufacturing processes are expected to conform to the environmental regulations of the country of origin.

Orders: please contact Bookpoint Ltd, 130 Milton Park, Abingdon, Oxon OX14 4SB. Telephone: +44 (0)1235 827720. Fax: +44 (0)1235 400454. Lines are open 9.00a.m.–5.00p.m., Monday to Saturday, with a 24-hour message answering service. Visit our website at www.hoddereducation.co.uk.

© Peter Clements
First published in 2012 by
Hodder Education,
An Hachette UK company
338 Euston Road
London NW1 3BH

Impression number   5 4 3 2
Year   2016 2015 2014 2013 2012

All rights reserved. Apart from any use permitted under UK copyright law, no part of this publication may be reproduced or transmitted in any form or by any means, electronic or mechanical, including photocopying and recording, or held within any information storage and retrieval system, without permission in writing from the publisher or under licence from the Copyright Licensing Agency Limited. Further details of such licences (for reprographic reproduction) may be obtained from the Copyright Licensing Agency Limited, Saffron House, 6–10 Kirby Street, London EC1N 8TS.

Cover photo © Tomislav Forgo – Fotolia
Typeset in 11/13 Stempel Schneidler by Pantek Media, Maidstone, Kent
Artwork by Pantek Media
Printed and bound in Spain
A catalogue record for this title is available from the British Library

ISBN 978 1 444 152 166

Contents

Introduction — 2

Section 1: Henry VIII and the quest for international influence — 6
- Henry's foreign policy aims 1509–11 — 6
- War against France and Scotland 1512–13 — 8
- England at Peace 1514–22 — 10
- Sidelined? England's foreign policy 1522–29 — 12
- The divorce and foreign policy — 14
- The search for a Protestant alliance 1539–40 — 16
- Exam focus — 18

Section 2: Structure of government — 24
- The rise of Thomas Wolsey — 24
- Wolsey as Cardinal and Papal legate — 26
- Wolsey as Lord Chancellor – the government of England 1509–29 — 28
- Relations with nobility and Parliament — 30
- Wolsey, Parliament and attempts to raise revenue — 32
- The fall of Wolsey 1529–30 — 34
- Exam focus — 36

Section 3: Henry's changing relations with the Catholic Church — 40
- The King's Great Matter — 40
- Attempts to obtain an annulment — 42
- From divorce to Royal Supremacy — 44
- The role of key individuals — 46
- Enforcing the Reformation — 48
- The Ten Articles and the Six Articles — 50
- Exam focus — 52

Section 4: The Dissolution of the Monasteries — 56
- The Visitations and the Valor Ecclesiasticus of 1535 — 56
- The dissolution of the smaller monasteries, 1536 — 58
- The Pilgrimage of Grace — 60
- The dissolution of the larger monasteries — 62
- Faction and political infighting in Henry's Court — 64
- Henry VIII – authority and religion — 66
- Exam focus — 68

Timeline — 72
Glossary — 74
Answers — 75

Introduction

About Unit 2

Unit 2 is worth 50 per cent of your AS level. It requires detailed knowledge of a period of British history and the ability to explore and analyse historical sources. Overall, 60 per cent of the marks available are awarded for source analysis (Assessment Objective 2), and 40 per cent for using own knowledge to form an explanation (Assessment Objective 1).

In the exam, you are required to answer one question with two parts. Part (a) is worth 20 marks and Part (b) is worth 40 marks. The exam lasts for 1 hour and 20 minutes, unless you have been awarded extra time. It is advisable to spend approximately one third of your time in the exam on Part (a) and the remaining two thirds on Part (b). There will be a choice of two Part (b) questions, of which you must answer one.

Part (a) tests your ability to:

- comprehend source material
- compare source material in detail, explaining how the sources agree and differ
- suggest reasons why the sources agree or differ based on their provenance
- reach an overall judgement.

Part (b) tests your ability to:

- select information that focuses on the question
- organise this information to provide an answer to the question
- integrate information from the sources and own knowledge
- weigh up evidence from sources and own knowledge to reach an overall judgement.

Henry VIII: Authority, Nation and Religion, 1509–40

The exam board specifies that students should study four general areas as part of this topic.

1. Henry VIII and the quest for international influence: relations with France, Scotland and Spain.
2. The structure of government: the role of Wolsey to 1529 and his relations with the King, nobility and Parliament.
3. Henry's changing relations with the Catholic Church and the break with Rome; the role of Parliament in the early stages of the Reformation; the roles of Cranmer and Cromwell.
4. The Dissolution of the Monasteries; support for and opposition to religious change from 1529.

How to use this book

This book has been designed to help you to develop the knowledge and skills necessary to succeed in the exam. The book is divided into four sections – one for each general area of the course. Each section is made up of a series of topics organised into double-page spreads. On the left-hand page, you will find a summary of the key content you need to learn. Words in bold in the key content are defined in the glossary (see page 74). On the right-hand page, you will find exam-focused activities. Together, these two strands of the book will take you through the knowledge and skills essential for exam success.

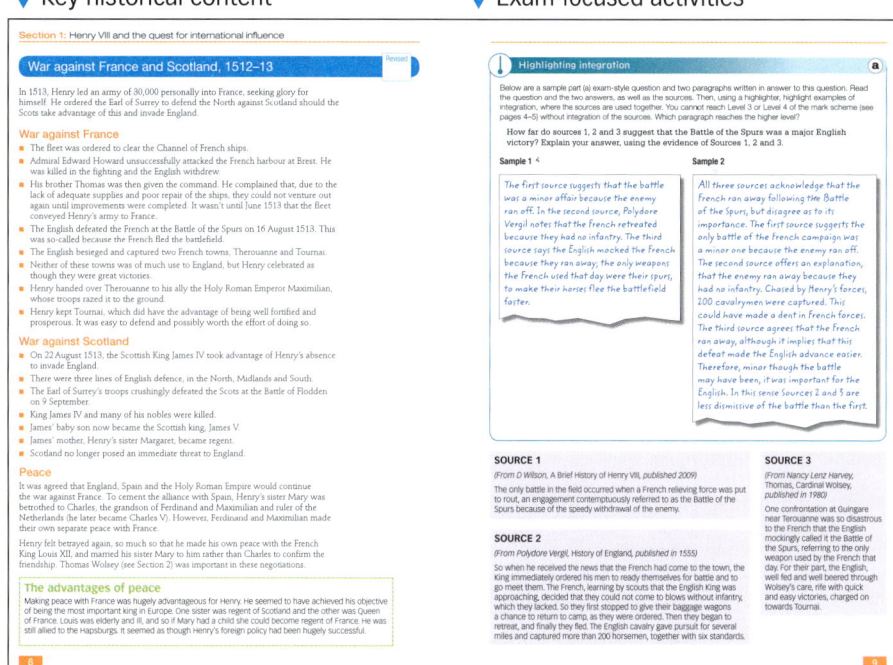

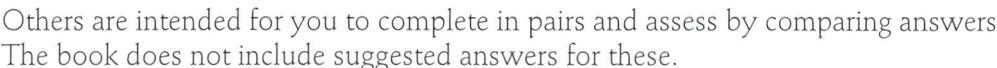

There are three levels of exam focused activities:

- Band 1 activities are designed to develop the foundational skills needed to pass the exam. These have a blue heading and this symbol:
- Band 2 activities are designed to build on the skills developed in Band 1 activities and to help you achieve a C grade. These have an orange heading and this symbol:
- Band 3 activities are designed to enable you to access the highest grades. These have a purple heading and this symbol:

Some of the activities have answers or suggested answers on pages 75–77 and have the following symbol to indicate this:

Others are intended for you to complete in pairs and assess by comparing answers. The book does not include suggested answers for these.

Each section ends with an exam-style question and model A-grade answer with examiner's commentary. This should give you guidance on what is required to achieve the top grades.

You can also keep track of your revision by ticking off each topic heading in the book, or by ticking the checklist on the contents page. Tick each box when you have:

- revised and understood a topic
- completed the activities.

3

Mark scheme

For some of the activities in the book it will be useful to refer to the mark scheme for the unit. Below is the mark scheme for Unit 2.

Part (a)

Level	Marks	Description
1	1–5	- Selects relevant material from the sources. - No attempt to compare the sources. - Sources are copied or paraphrased. *Level 1 answers are highly simplistic.*
2	6–10	- Selects relevant material from the sources. - Notes similarities and differences between the sources. - Simple conclusions about provenance. *Level 2 answers have some focus on the question, but significant weaknesses. For example, comparisons may be superficial or the answer may demonstrate some misunderstanding of the sources.*
3	11–15	- Selects relevant information from the sources. - Detailed comparison of similarities and differences. - Begins to use provenance to explain similarities and differences between accounts. - Begins to answer 'how far …?'. *Level 3 answers address the question and demonstrate a good understanding of how the sources agree and differ.*
4	16–20	- Selects relevant information from the sources. - Detailed comparison of similarities and differences. - Provenance is used to explain similarities and differences between accounts and to weigh up the evidence. - Sustained focus on 'how far …?'. *Level 4 answers clearly answer the question and demonstrate a sophisticated understanding of the evidence of the sources in their historical context.*

Part (b)

AO1: Using historical knowledge to form an explanation

Level	Marks	Description
1	1–6	• General points with limited focus on the question. • Inaccurate supporting evidence. • No integration of sources and own knowledge.
2	7–12	• General points with some focus on the question. • Accurate and relevant – but generalised – supporting evidence. • Attempts integration of sources and own knowledge.
3	13–18	• General points with secure focus on the question. • Mostly accurate and relevant supporting evidence. • Some integration of sources and own knowledge.
4	19–24	• General points with strong focus on the question. • Accurate and relevant supporting evidence. • Integration of sources and own knowledge.

AO2: Analysing source material

Level	Marks	Description
1	1–4	• Copied or paraphrased information from the sources. • Little focus on the question.
2	5–8	• Information from the sources is summarised and used to provide a simple answer to the question.
3	9–12	• Evidence from the sources is selected to support and challenge the view expressed in the question.
4	13–16	• As Level 3 • Weighs the evidence of the sources and uses this in reaching an overall judgement.

Section 1: Henry VIII and the quest for international influence

Henry's foreign policy aims, 1509–11

Revised

Henry VIII planned a more adventurous policy than his cautious father. Henry VII (r. 1485–1509) had sought stability abroad to enable him to consolidate his own rule at home and had allied England with Spain, an arrangement Henry VIII confirmed by marrying Catherine of Aragon in 1509. She was the daughter of the Spanish King Ferdinand, and the widow of Henry VIII's brother Arthur.

Foreign policy dominated the first twenty years of Henry VIII's reign. He had **imperial ideas** involving re-conquest of lands, particularly in France, and making England a major power in Europe.

The reasons for the dominance of foreign policy were:

- England had governed much of France during the Middle Ages. Henry wanted to win back French territories lost during the previous century. He referred to himself as the King of England and France.
- Henry was young and virile. He found war glamorous and wanted to assert himself as a dashing soldier-king. His heroes included Henry V, who had won the battle of Agincourt in 1415, and the mythological King Arthur. He wanted his court to be associated with Camelot.
- Henry wanted England to be politically at the heart of Europe, not just a small nation on the periphery. He believed he could exploit the rivalry between the superpowers of Spain (ruled by the Hapsburgs) and France (ruled by the House of Valois) to develop England's importance.

European context

Europe was dominated by the powers of Spain, France and the **Holy Roman Empire**. They were increasingly coming into conflict in Italy, the home of the papacy. As well as being leader of the Roman Catholic Church, the Pope ruled vast territories in Italy and sought to increase his dominions. In 1508, France had intervened to save Venice from papal attack. Pope Julius II then called for a 'Holy League' to expel France from Italy. England and Spain joined this league, and Henry prepared to attack France.

The First French War, 1511–12

- Henry believed King Ferdinand of Spain would help England win back **Aquitaine** in France. An English force under the Marquis of Dorset invaded at Guyenne in south-western France, but the promised Spanish help never arrived.
- Ferdinand used the English invasion as a diversion while he conquered Navarre. This was an important route for both trade and pilgrims. Its control was far more important to him than helping the English win back lands in France.
- Without supplies and unable to advance, Dorset's troops began to die of dysentery in vast numbers. The commander had little choice but to retreat and head for home.
- Ferdinand made peace with France, and Henry felt betrayed.
- Back in England, Dorset found that Ferdinand had accused him of incompetence. If Henry agreed, it may have been because he didn't want to upset his father-in-law, whose help he knew he would need again. He had, however, learnt that allies couldn't necessarily be trusted.

Henry's first taste of war had ended without success.

Support or challenge?

Below is a sample exam-style part (a) question which asks how far the sources agree with a specific statement. Below this are a series of sources. Decide whether the sources support or challenge the statement in the question.

> How far do the sources agree that the main reason Henry VIII went to war in 1511 was to help expel the French from Italy?
>
> Explain your answer using the evidence of Sources 1, 2 and 3.

SOURCE 1

(From Nancy Lenz Harvey, Thomas Cardinal Wolsey, *published 1980)*

The purpose of the Holy League was so that 'the French king shall not nor may not attain to his cruel purpose for to destroy all the country of Italy'.

SOURCE 2

(From D Wilson, A Brief History of Henry VIII, *published 2009)*

Ferdinand would supply his son-in-law (Henry) with cavalry, cannon and wagons and help him to claw back the territory of Aquitaine, which had once been annexed to the English Throne.

SOURCE 3

(From JJ Scarisbrick, Henry VIII, *published 1968)*

It was clear that Ferdinand was never interested in winning anything for his son-in-law and had always intended to use the English troops to cover the seizure by his own army of the independent kingdom of Navarre.

Spot the mistake

Below is part of an answer to the question in 'Support or challenge' above. Why does this paragraph not get into Level 4? Once you have identified the mistake, rewrite the paragraph so it displays the qualities of Level 4. The mark scheme on pages 4–5 will help you.

> Source 1 tells me that the purpose of the Holy League was so that 'the French king shall not nor may not attain to his cruel purpose for to destroy all the country of Italy'. Source 2 says that Ferdinand would supply his son-in-law (Henry) with cavalry, cannon and wagons and help him to win back the territory of Aquitaine, which had once been annexed to the English Throne. Source 3 says it was clear that Ferdinand was never interested in winning anything for his son-in-law and had always intended to use the English troops to cover the seizure by his own army of the independent kingdom of Navarre. All these sources give different reasons for Henry going to war. However, I think that he wanted glory. His heroes were fighting kings like Henry V and King Arthur. He was only young and tried to make his court like Camelot. No one would believe how courageous he was if he didn't go to war. So there were different reasons for him going to war against France. It wasn't just to expel the French from Italy.

Section 1: Henry VIII and the quest for international influence

War against France and Scotland, 1512–13

In 1513, Henry led an army of 30,000 personally into France, seeking glory for himself. He ordered the Earl of Surrey to defend the North against Scotland should the Scots take advantage of this and invade England.

War against France
- The fleet was ordered to clear the Channel of French ships.
- Admiral Edward Howard unsuccessfully attacked the French harbour at Brest. He was killed in the fighting and the English withdrew.
- His brother Thomas was then given the command. He complained that, due to the lack of adequate supplies and poor repair of the ships, they could not venture out again until improvements were completed. It wasn't until June 1513 that the fleet conveyed Henry's army to France.
- The English defeated the French at the Battle of the Spurs on 16 August 1513. This was so-called because the French fled the battlefield.
- The English besieged and captured two French towns, Therouanne and Tournai.
- Neither of these towns was of much use to England, but Henry celebrated as though they were great victories.
- Henry handed over Therouanne to his ally the Holy Roman Emperor Maximilian, whose troops razed it to the ground.
- Henry kept Tournai, which did have the advantage of being well fortified and prosperous. It was easy to defend and possibly worth the effort of doing so.

War against Scotland
- On 22 August 1513, the Scottish King James IV took advantage of Henry's absence to invade England.
- There were three lines of English defence, in the North, Midlands and South.
- The Earl of Surrey's troops crushingly defeated the Scots at the Battle of Flodden on 9 September.
- King James IV and many of his nobles were killed.
- James' baby son now became the Scottish king, James V.
- James' mother, Henry's sister Margaret, became regent.
- Scotland no longer posed an immediate threat to England.

Peace

It was agreed that England, Spain and the Holy Roman Empire would continue the war against France. To cement the alliance with Spain, Henry's sister Mary was betrothed to Charles, the grandson of Ferdinand and Maximilian and ruler of the Netherlands (he later became Charles V). However, Ferdinand and Maximilian made their own separate peace with France.

Henry felt betrayed again, so much so that he made his own peace with the French King Louis XII, and married his sister Mary to him rather than Charles to confirm the friendship. Thomas Wolsey (see Section 2) was important in these negotiations.

> ### The advantages of peace
> Making peace with France was hugely advantageous for Henry. He seemed to have achieved his objective of being the most important king in Europe. One sister was regent of Scotland and the other was Queen of France. Louis was elderly and ill, and so if Mary had a child she could become regent of France. He was still allied to the Hapsburgs. It seemed as though Henry's foreign policy had been hugely successful.

8

Highlighting integration

Below are a sample part (a) exam-style question and two paragraphs written in answer to this question. Read the question and the two answers, as well as the sources. Then, using a highlighter, highlight examples of integration, where the sources are used together. You cannot reach Level 3 or Level 4 of the mark scheme (see pages 4–5) without integration of the sources. Which paragraph reaches the higher level?

How far do sources 1, 2 and 3 suggest that the Battle of the Spurs was a major English victory? Explain your answer, using the evidence of Sources 1, 2 and 3.

Sample 1

> The first source suggests that the battle was a minor affair because the enemy ran off. In the second source, Polydore Vergil notes that the French retreated because they had no infantry. The third source says the English mocked the French because they ran away; the only weapons the French used that day were their spurs, to make their horses flee the battlefield faster.

Sample 2

> All three sources acknowledge that the French ran away following the Battle of the Spurs, but disagree as to its importance. The first source suggests the only battle of the French campaign was a minor one because the enemy ran off. The second source offers an explanation, that the enemy ran away because they had no infantry. Chased by Henry's forces, 200 cavalrymen were captured. This could have made a dent in French forces. The third source agrees that the French ran away, although it implies that this defeat made the English advance easier. Therefore, minor though the battle may have been, it was important for the English. In this sense Sources 2 and 3 are less dismissive of the battle than the first.

SOURCE 1

(From D Wilson, A Brief History of Henry VIII, published 2009)

The only battle in the field occurred when a French relieving force was put to rout, an engagement contemptuously referred to as the Battle of the Spurs because of the speedy withdrawal of the enemy.

SOURCE 2

(From Polydore Vergil, History of England, published in 1555)

So when he received the news that the French had come to the town, the King immediately ordered his men to ready themselves for battle and to go meet them. The French, learning by scouts that the English King was approaching, decided that they could not come to blows without infantry, which they lacked. So they first stopped to give their baggage wagons a chance to return to camp, as they were ordered. Then they began to retreat, and finally they fled. The English cavalry gave pursuit for several miles and captured more than 200 horsemen, together with six standards.

SOURCE 3

(From Nancy Lenz Harvey, Thomas, Cardinal Wolsey, published in 1980)

One confrontation at Guingare near Terouanne was so disastrous to the French that the English mockingly called it the Battle of the Spurs, referring to the only weapon used by the French that day. For their part, the English, well fed and well beered through Wolsey's care, rife with quick and easy victories, charged on towards Tournai.

Section 1: Henry VIII and the quest for international influence

England at peace 1514–22

With his sisters respectively regent of Scotland and Queen of France, Henry's international standing seemed assured. Yet by 1514, things started to unravel:

- In France, Louis XII died.
- His successor Francis I sought to renew the conflict with Spain.
- His sister Margaret was stripped of the Scottish regency after marrying the Earl of Angus, and fled to England.

The importance of the Treaty of London

The Treaty of London was signed in October 1518 between England, France, Portugal, Spain, Denmark, Hungary, the Swiss Republic and various German states.

- It was a non-aggression pact. Those signing agreed to help each other if any were attacked.
- The Treaty was seen at the time as a great political achievement. It was an example of **collective security**, a sincere attempt to banish war.
- It seemed to place England at the centre of European affairs, with Henry and Wolsey seen as leading figures.

Changing relations between Henry, Charles V and Francis I

- In October 1518, Henry sold Tournai back to France for 12,000 **livres**.
- Charles V succeeded as Holy Roman Emperor in 1519. As ruler of both Spain and the Netherlands, his territories encircled France. Henry sought to act as the arbiter between Charles and Francis.

Chancellor Wolsey was the prime mover in policies aimed at achieving lasting peace. Both he and Henry knew there was little enthusiasm within the country for more costly wars. Henry sought to maintain his international influence through becoming the major peace broker in Europe. However, in trying to play off Charles V against King Francis I of France, he often forgot that they were using him in the same way.

Defender of the Faith

In response to Martin Luther's **Ninety-five theses** attacking corruption inside the Catholic Church, Henry wrote the Defence of the Seven Sacraments, asserting the power of the Roman Catholic faith. In gratitude the Pope gave him the title Defender of the Faith. As a result, Henry saw himself as a major theologian and defender of Catholicism against attack.

Field of the Cloth of Gold

- Henry met Francis I at the Field of the Cloth of Gold, near Calais, France, in June 1520. The two young monarchs tried to outdo each other in splendour. However, despite assurances of eternal friendship, this meeting came to nothing. A Venetian observer spoke for many in observing, 'These kings are not at peace … they detest each other cordially.'
- Henry left the Field of the Cloth of Gold for talks with Charles V. Charles tried to drive Henry away from friendship with France, but was preoccupied with problems within his own dominions.

The end of the peace

In 1521, Francis attacked Navarre and Luxembourg. On 25 August 1521, Henry signed a secret treaty with Charles V in which he promised to help Charles in his war with France at some future date, when he could afford it. Both sought 'The Great Enterprise,' the downfall of France, but neither monarch trusted the other.

Delete as applicable

Below are a sample exam-style part (b) question and a paragraph written in answer to this question. Read the paragraph and decide which of the possible options (in bold) is most appropriate. Delete the least appropriate options and complete the paragraph by justifying your selection.

Henry VIII succeeded in the years 1514–22 in becoming the arbiter of Europe.

Do you agree with this statement? Explain your answer using Sources 1 and 2 and your own knowledge.

> Sources 1 and 2 suggest that if Henry was the arbiter of Europe it was more to do with the influence of Wolsey than his own effort, although he took the credit. Source 2 for example suggests that Wolsey's success reflected well on Henry's court. Source 1 focuses on the Treaty of London, which was seen as Wolsey's towering achievement. However, the success of Henry and Wolsey wasn't inevitable. Louis XII had died, and Henry's sister Mary had been forced to leave France. He realised that taxpayers were unwilling to finance another war. He therefore sought to increase his influence by acting as a power broker. For example, Wolsey organised the Treaty of London in 1518, which many saw as a triumph for Henry. In addition Henry, distrusting Charles, had on Wolsey's advice began to make moves towards friendship with France. This was achieved at the Field of Cloth of Gold in 1520. This made Charles V try to play Henry off against Francis, although he was preoccupied with events in Germany. In fact it seemed that Henry had achieved friendship with France while Charles was neutralised by these problems. On the basis of this diplomacy, Henry must have thought that he had **achieved/almost achieved/not achieved** his objective of becoming arbiter of Europe, because
>
> _____
>
> _____

SOURCE 1

(From J Ross, The Tudors, *published 1979)*

England had become a power to be reckoned with – if not the equal of mighty France and Spain, at least the makeweight that could tip the balance between them. Wolsey was proud of his own contribution. 'Nothing pleases him more than to be called the arbiter of the affairs of Christendom,' noted the Venetian Ambassador after the Treaty of London had been signed. This great treaty, completed in the autumn of 1518, was the consummation of all Wolsey had worked towards. All the great powers and lesser nations such as the Danes, the Portuguese and the Swiss, subscribed to an international peace agreement signed in London which overrode all previous treaties and made provision for perpetual peace in Europe.

SOURCE 2

(From Nancy Lenz Harvey, Thomas Wolsey, *published 1980)*

[Wolsey] was now the head of negotiation. It was the point on which the heads of every state in Europe agreed. As a result the man from Ipswich found himself sought by every foreign ambassador to the court of England. And Henry, feeling himself as triumphant in the field of diplomacy as he had been on the fields of battle, looked at his friend and minister and embraced him. Between them there was neither envy nor duplicity, and the King delighted that his minister was fast becoming the first minister of all Europe. The glory of that recognition reflected on the court of England.

Section 1: Henry VIII and the quest for international influence

Sidelined? England's foreign policy, 1522–29

The period of the mid-1520s saw England increasingly sidelined and having to react to European events over which it had little control.

In 1523, circumstances in Europe changed. The Duc de Bourbon, Constable of France, rebelled against Francis. He looked to Henry and Charles for support. Hoping to win the throne of France for himself, Henry sent an invasion force of 100,000 led by the Duke of Suffolk. Charles was meant to send reinforcements from the Netherlands, but let Henry down. England was left alone to fight the French in France. Charles was more interested in securing his frontier in the Pyrenees and continuing the war in Northern Italy. Suffolk had begun to march on Paris. However, as the weather worsened, he retreated back to Calais.

At this point, even Henry had lost enthusiasm for war. Wolsey was more interested in becoming 'the arbiter of the affairs of Christendom.' He had set his eyes on the papacy, and favoured peace. England was still allied with Charles, who continued his war with France. However, there were specific reasons why England couldn't afford to go to war in the mid-1520s:

- The cost was too great. Attempts to raise money were disappointing and the failed Amicable Grant of 1525 (see page 32) almost led to rebellion.
- So far, the results of war had been disappointing. Henry had little to show for England's efforts.
- Henry would be expected to provide supplies and equipment for Charles V's army. It was relatively easy for France to intercept these in transit.

It could be argued that it all came down to money. However, in 1525 everything changed again. Increasingly anxious to secure his dynasty with an heir, Henry was beginning to contemplate divorce. Yet his wife Catherine of Aragon was Charles V's aunt, so Charles would be unlikely to support Henry.

Relationships with Charles V

Renewed war between Charles and Francis led to the capture of Francis after the battle of Pavia. Henry felt he could share in the spoils of victory without having to go to war. Charles, however, ignored Henry's requests in the peace negotiations. He thought Henry had let him down. He married Isabella of Portugal instead of Princess Mary.

The breakdown of relations with Charles put even more strain on Henry's marriage. In spring 1527 he told Wolsey he wanted an annulment. Wolsey, who had always favoured friendship with France, believed this would lead to an irrevocable rift with Charles, so began to promote a French alliance.

Events in Europe again overtook English plans. In 1526, Wolsey organised the League of Cognac between Italian states and France, aimed at resisting Charles' intervention in Italy. While England didn't join, it did offer financial aid. However, Charles' troops proved unstoppable. Under the Duc de Bourbon, they invaded Rome on 6 May 1527 and subjected the city to immense slaughter. The Pope fled to his fortress, the Castel San Angelo. The Venetians asked Henry to intervene. However by this time he was too preoccupied by the 'Great Matter' of his divorce.

Spectrum of significance

Below is a list of reasons why Henry did not go to war in the mid-1520s. Indicate their relative importance by writing their numbers on the spectrum below and justify your placement, explaining why some factors are more important than others.

1. Henry was horrified by the slaughter in warfare.
2. England couldn't afford to go to war and taxpayers were reluctant to give subsidies.
3. Henry distrusted his allies who had let him down time and time again.
4. Henry distrusted the ability of his commanders.
5. Henry did not wish to disrupt England's continental trade.
6. Henry had decided to divorce Catherine of Aragon and was afraid of how Charles V would respond.
7. Henry preferred to supply allies who would do his fighting for him.

Very important   Less important

Write the question

The following sources relate to Henry's role as a peacemaker in Europe. Read the information on the page opposite. Having done this, write an exam-style part (a) question using the sources.

SOURCE 1

(Cardinal Campeggio to Henry VIII)

The Pope, who is in great trouble, is sending to England, the Bishop of Worcester to inform the King of recent occurrences at which he was present. All his hope at this critical time is on the King. All Christendom is in danger from the Turk, now that the King of Hungary has been defeated and slain.

SOURCE 2

(Wolsey to Henry VIII, 9 October 1526)

… urges the King to give the Pope for the maintenance of 5000 Swiss and 400 men at arms, 30,000 or 35,000 ducats by which he may forbear to enter the League and mediate more effectively with the Emperor … King Henry will secure peace, have the gratitude of the Pope and the League [of Cognac], save his treasure, preserve his amity with the Emperor; and thus by his wise counsel, Christendom may attend to the debellation [destruction] of the Turks.

SOURCE 3

(Cardinal Campeggio to Wolsey, Rome, 22 October 1526)

They have much confidence in the King as the author of peace between Christian princes and the champion of the Liberty of Christendom. The Pope's thoughts are all concentrated on the means of defending the Lord's flock committed to his charge. The fleet of the Spanish viceroy is hourly expected from Spain and if it comes and finds the Pope unprepared, total ruin will ensue.

Section 1: Henry VIII and the quest for international influence

The divorce and foreign policy

Henry's desire for a divorce meant he could no longer be allied to Charles V. The problem was compounded by the fact that only the Pope could grant a divorce and, after the invasion of Rome, he was effectively Charles' prisoner. Henry feared an invasion by Charles. However Charles' own room for manoeuvre was limited:

- Charles was worried about the encroachment of Turkey into eastern Europe, including some of the lands he ruled as Holy Roman Emperor.
- He was also concerned about Germany, where many states were now adopting the Protestant faith.
- He could have applied economic sanctions against Henry. Yet this would have hurt his subjects in the Netherlands, who were increasingly dependent on English trade, particularly in the manufacture and sale of textiles.

Charles' armies meanwhile continued their success in Italy. The French were defeated at the battle of Landriano on June 29, 1529. Peace was made at Cambrai. Wolsey had wanted to be present there so he could influence negotiations, but Henry had insisted he remain at home at the **Legatine Court**, trying to arrange the divorce (see page 42).

Henry became preoccupied by seeking support for the divorce abroad. Wolsey had fallen from power in 1529, having failed to achieve the divorce. He had asked foreign universities for judgements and some, particularly after bribes, were favourable. However, as a previous Pope had given his dispensation for Henry to marry Catherine of Aragon, the former wife of his deceased brother Arthur, only the present Pope had the authority to rescind this and declare the marriage invalid. When the Pope did finally make a decision on the divorce in July 1533, it was that Henry should remain married to Catherine.

Relations with France

Henry again looked to France for support. The two kings met at Calais in October 1532, where Anne Boleyn was effectively treated as queen. Henry may even have had Francis' support for the divorce, and Francis was trying to make an alliance with the Pope.

By the time the two had met in Marseille in October 1533, with Francis suggesting an alliance of France, England and the Pope against Charles, Henry had put himself beyond papal support by declaring the marriage invalid himself and marrying Anne Boleyn. Meanwhile in 1534, Pope Clement VII died. His successor Paul III was friendlier with France and may have been more sympathetic to Henry's desire for a divorce.

However, events had moved on again, with the **Reformation** developing in England and Henry regarded as a pariah in Catholic Europe. Nevertheless, the death of Catherine of Aragon in 1536 made war less likely, as Charles no longer had a personal interest in invasion. Moreover, Charles and Francis became embroiled in a dispute as to who should succeed to the Duchy of Milan, which made them too preoccupied to threaten England. Henry hoped he could revert to his role as a peacemaker.

Mind map

Use the information on the opposite page and your own knowledge to add detail to the mind map below to show how each power faced problems which impacted on their reactions to Henry's desire for a divorce from Catherine of Aragon.

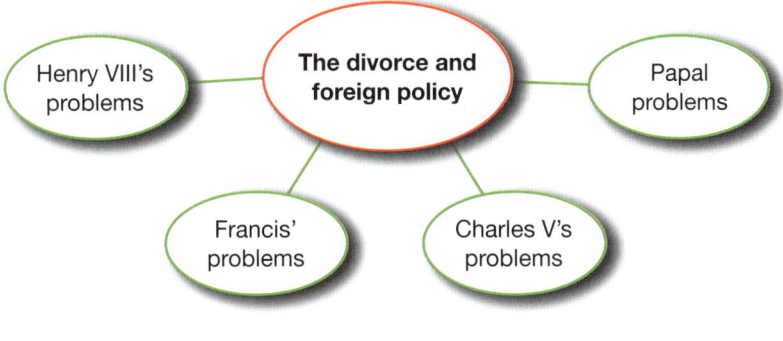

Add own knowledge

Below are a sample exam-style part (b) question and the two sources referred to in the question. In one colour, draw links between the sources to show ways in which they agree about whether the invasion threat was real. In another colour, draw links between the sources to show ways in which they disagree. Then around the edge of the sources write in your own relevant knowledge. Again, draw links to show the ways in which this agrees and disagrees with the sources.

> Do you agree with the view that the threat of invasion from Spain was 'very small indeed'? Explain your answer using Sources 1 and 2 and your own knowledge.

SOURCE 1

(From M D Palmer, Henry VIII *second edition, published 1984)*

The danger of intervention by Charles V on behalf of his aunt was very small indeed. Between the siege of Vienna by the Turks in 1529 and his successful conquest of the Turkish base in Tunis in 1535, Charles was obsessed by the threat of the Turks to Hungary and to his naval power in the Western Mediterranean. He had to shelve the German problem by conceding religious toleration to the German princes of the **Schmalkaldic League** at the Diet of Nuremberg in 1532. It was unlikely therefore that Henry's treatment of Catherine and the subsequent break with Rome would command much of his attention.

Given the chance of promoting war between England and the mighty empire of her nephew Charles in order to re-establish her marital rights, Catherine chose peace. Charles may have been unwilling, [but] Chapuys [The Spanish Ambassador] seemed convinced he could be pushed into it if Catherine encouraged her English supporters to rise against Henry.

SOURCE 2

(Letter from Mendoza, Imperial Ambassador)

Everyone feels so strongly about what is being said about setting the Queen aside, both for her sake and because the Princess [Mary] would end up a bastard, should it really happen, and six or seven thousand men landed on the coast of Cornwall to espouse the cause of both mother and daughter, then forty thousand Englishmen would join them.

Section 1: Henry VIII and the quest for international influence

The search for a Protestant Alliance, 1539–40

Revised

In 1535, the Pope had **excommunicated** Henry and called for his removal. Henry again feared invasion, particularly as France controlled the entire European coastline opposite southern England and was building a large navy at its shipyards in Brest and Havre de Grave. In response, Henry:

- developed the English navy. In 1514 he had 29 ships, by 1539 he had 120 in the mouth of the Thames and 30 in Portsmouth
- began to develop coastal defences, often with building materials recycled from nearby monasteries
- offered himself as husband to various French princesses to cement a new French alliance. When this came to nothing, he wooed Christina Duchess of Milan, a niece of Charles V
- **mustered levies**, in March 1539 in the south-eastern regions to fight a possible invasion.

Other attempts of seeking alliance through marriage having failed, Thomas Cromwell persuaded Henry he should seek a Protestant alliance. In 1539, he began talks with the Schmalkaldic League. However, with the passing of the Six Articles (see page 50) which meant the English Church remained Catholic in theology despite its split from Rome, little came of these talks – except the marriage with Anne of Cleves.

Marriage with Anne of Cleves

Cleves was a German duchy in an important strategic position astride the River Rhine. The Duke, William, was in dispute with Charles V over the ownership of Guelderland in Holland. William therefore needed allies, as did Henry. His sister Anne of Cleves was offered to Henry as his wife to cement an alliance. However, as tensions eased, Henry realised he no longer needed this alliance. Indeed, he could get dragged into conflicts in which England had no interest. For this reason, as well as incompatibility, he divorced Anne of Cleves soon after having married her.

Later developments

Henry took charge of foreign policy himself as the 1540s developed. This saw him again making war on France and seeking further alliances with Charles. In 1543 he invaded France and captured Boulogne. Again, his ally let him down. Charles and Francis made a truce, which saw English troops isolated and forced to retreat to Calais. In 1545, France was prevented by adverse weather conditions from attempting an English invasion. In the same year, Henry was also at war with Scotland, hoping but failing to turn it into an English puppet state.

Henry had attempted to turn England into a major European power, either by war or as a major power broker between the Valois and Hapsburg monarchs. Too often his allies let him down. With religious wars dominating on the continent, England may after all have remained on the periphery.

Eliminate irrelevance

Below are a sample exam-style part (b) question and a paragraph written in answer to it. Read the paragraph and identify parts of the paragraph that are not directly relevant to the question. Draw a line through the information that is irrelevant and justify your deletions in the margin.

Do you agree with the view that Henry VIII sought a Protestant alliance because of his continuing fear of an invasion by the French? Explain your answer using Sources 1 and 2 and your own knowledge.

> Henry's main reason for seeking a Protestant alliance was his continuing fear of French invasion. Sources 1 and 2 both show that the invasion threat was real and Henry needed powerful friends. Source 1 shows that Henry was vulnerable to attack because he had been excommunicated and France and Spain were now friends. Source 2 goes further, suggesting that Catholic superpowers are preparing to invade England. Cromwell was singled out in particular as a bad influence. The Pope didn't like him because he had organised the reformation and dissolution of the monasteries. The fear of invasion by France was growing because France controlled the entire European coastline opposite southern England and was building a large navy at its shipyards in Brest and Havre de Grave. Henry's marriage to Anne of Cleves, whose brother was an important German prince, helped cement Henry's Protestant alliance. Henry hoped that France would not invade England if Germany would come to his aid. However, he didn't find Anne of Cleves very attractive and tried to get out of the marriage. Anne was unsophisticated and a bit dumpy. Her German clothes didn't flatter her. But he couldn't just end the relationship for fear of upsetting her brother.

SOURCE 1

(From J Ross, The Tudors, *published 1979)*

By taking a foreign wife [Anne of Cleves], Henry intended to secure a much needed ally abroad. England's isolation in 1538 was potentially dangerous; not only did Spain and France, who had been at war, mend their differences, but the Pope at last took definite action against Henry by excommunicating him. Now he was officially fair game for any Christian who wished to attack him, and even his own subjects were absolved of their obedience to him. The King of England needed all the powerful friends he could get.

SOURCE 2

(From R Hutchinson, Thomas Cromwell, *published 2007)*

The Catholic monarchs of Spain and France were urged to unite to return England to papal authority and Cromwell, 'that limb of Satan' was singled out personally to be cast into hell's all consuming fire … the forces of the Catholic Church were at least being marshalled to attack England's recalcitrant and egotistical monarch. Both were terribly vulnerable to invasion by the European superpowers.

Recommended reading

Below is a list of suggested further reading to help develop your understanding of foreign affairs:
- M D Palmer, *Henry VIII*, Longman second edition, pages 12–14 and 63–75, (1984)
- Glenn Richardson, *Good Friends and Brothers? Francis I and Henry VIII*, History Today 44, (1994)
- Jez Ross, *Henry VIII's Early Foreign Policy 1509–29*, History Review 41, (2001)
- Derek Wilson, *A Brief History of Henry VIII*, Robinson, Chapters 3 and 4, (2009)
- www.historylearningsite.co.uk/henry_viii_foreign_policy.htm

Section 1: Henry VIII and the quest for international influence

Section 1: Exam focus

Revised

On pages 20–23 are sample A-grade answers to the exam-style questions on these two pages. Read the answers and the examiner's comments around them.

a) How far do these sources agree that supplying the troops was a significant problem for Henry in the French War of 1513? Explain your answer using the evidence of Sources 1, 2 and 3.

b) Do you agree with the view that Scotland remained a threat to England between the years 1509–40? Explain your answer using Sources 4, 5 and 6 and your own knowledge.

SOURCE 1

(Memorandum from Richard Fox, Bishop of Winchester in 1514. He was responding to Henry's concern about the lack of hay during the 1513 campaign)

When the King was at Calais with his army, not only the corn and hay but the grass on the ground was consumed and destroyed so that at the King's returning thither there was no provision for hay for the horses.

SOURCE 2

(Memorandum from Thomas Wolsey in 1513. Wolsey is listing the provisions necessary for the English troops in France)

1. The tonnage of fifty ships to come from Spain and victuals for three months – eight thousand pounds.
2. As many ships of England and Flanders of like portage for 'transporting over of the King' and one thousand men – eight thousand pounds.
3. One hundred thirty two ships of sixty-one hundred tons for conveyancing victuals from the Thames to Hampton for three months – thirty-five hundred pounds.
4. Victuals for the King and ten thousand men for two months – eighty-six hundred pounds.

SOURCE 3

(Richard Fox, Bishop of Winchester, writing in 1513 about the problem of transporting provisions across the Channel to the English Army in France)

As for sending of ships for the scouring of the narrow sea and escorting the horses that go to Calais, I pray God send you them in time; for it is too great a shame to lose the ships that be lost. And I trust you will no more adventure neither the ordinance, artillery, victuals nor men until you have escort ships.

SOURCE 4

(From M D Palmer, Henry VIII, *second edition, published 1984)*

Scotland presented a great threat to Henry throughout his reign, especially when he was at war with France. When war broke out between France and England in 1513, James IV of Scotland felt much more loyalty to the Auld Alliance than to the more recent marriage treaty with England ... The result of James' intervention in this war was his defeat and death at Flodden in 1513.

[Margaret] gave up the regency to the Duke of Albany ... Albany was far more French than Scottish in outlook and his governorship of Scotland from 1515 to 1524 was a time of worry for Henry. Cromwell, in a speech he prepared for the 1523 parliament, named Scotland as the first priority of English foreign policy. He wanted it subdued and then united to England.

It was the marriage of James V, first in 1537 to Madeleine, daughter of Francis I and on her death to Mary of Guise in 1538 that reopened the Scottish problem.

SOURCE 5

(From D Wilson, A Brief History of Henry VIII, *published 2009)*

[Flodden] was one of the major turning points in Anglo-Scottish relations. For the rest of Henry's reign the demoralised Scots were in no position to intervene effectively in affairs south of the border.

SOURCE 6

(From a speech from Thomas Cromwell to Parliament in 1523)

... if it would please his magnanimous courage to convert first and chief of his whole intent and purpose, not only to the overrunning and subduing of Scotland but also to join the same realm unto his, so that both they and we might live under one law and policy forever ... of this act should follow the highest abashment to the said Francis that ever happened to him ... it is but a simpleness for us to think to keep possessions in France, which is severed from us by the ocean sea and suffer Scotland, joined unto us by nature in all one island, unto which we may have recourse at all times when we will, which also to subdue.

Section 1: Henry VIII and the quest for international influence

a) How far do these sources agree that supplying the troops was a significant problem for Henry in the French War of 1513? Explain your answer using the evidence of Sources 1, 2 and 3.

Annotation	Answer
The sources are compared and integrated in the answer at the outset.	While all three sources would appear to agree that supplying English troops with sufficient supplies and equipment presented problems, Source 2 shows to some extent how the problem was dealt with. This takes the issue further to suggest that there were solutions to these problems.
Source provenance.	All the sources date from the period, with the second from Wolsey himself showing the extent of the provisioning while the first and second highlight the problems.
Examples given in support.	In the first source Fox is writing a year after the event to show with hindsight how important it is to provide enough fodder while in the third he is drawing attention to problems with transportation across the Channel. We will examine the sources to analyse how far they do agree that the problems were significant in terms of the subject focus of each.
Refers to all three sources comparatively, while adding how Source 3 develops a further point.	On the surface then, all three sources suggest that there were problems supplying English troops during the French War. Sources 1 and 2 refer to the need for logistics in supplying and equipping the army sent by Henry to France. Source 1 is more concerned with the problem resulting from lack of fodder for the amount of horses that would need to be sent, while Source 2 shows how organised Wolsey was as Royal Almoner. Source 3 tends to concentrate on another problem with supply — that of transporting the army and its supplies safely across the continent. However all show that supplies were a huge problem. In Source 3, for example, it states that one couldn't risk losing the equipment or men who were crossing the Channel.
Recognises that the provisions may not get to their destination and ties this into Source 3.	The first source relates specifically to providing sufficient food for the horses — it says that all the grass in the immediate area had been eaten in addition to the grain, much of which would have necessarily been brought over from England. This could support Source 3, which mentions the difficulty of Channel crossing, and indeed that some ships had already been lost. Both Sources 1 and 3 agree that supplying the provisions is a problem, while the third also suggests it is dangerous because of hostile enemy ships in the Channel.
	However, there is also evidence that supplying the troops was not a significant problem during the war. The second source refers to the sheer scale and cost of supply. The third item for example speaks of 132 ships with three months' worth of supply costing £3500. Clearly a long war could be very costly indeed. However, Wolsey has prepared for this as best he could. It isn't as though the invasion was going to be lacking in

provisions – at least in theory. Again the fact the provisions have left England does not mean that they will arrive safely for the English army in France – which brings us back to the point made in Source 3. However, lack of supply could stop the success of the invasion – without fodder for example the horses would starve, while without food and other provisions soldiers would have to live off the land, assuming the land could sustain them. It would also cause problems with local people and mean they had less time to fight. Soldiers would fight more efficiently if they didn't have to worry about provisioning themselves.

While all three sources show that supply was a huge issue, they each take a different aspect – the first on fodder for horses, the third on crossing the Channel safely, while the second shows that Wolsey is attempting to meet the demand for provisions. It also hints at the scale necessary – as does the first by showing that horses have eaten all the grass in addition to fodder provided.

Source 2 suggests that while supply is a big issue it may not actually be a huge problem because Wolsey has organised the provision on a grand scale. Therefore its tone may be more congratulatory, suggesting he wanted to impress the King by how well he is prepared and the amount of provisions he has procured. The third source has more than a hint of desperation – 'I pray God send you them in time; for it is too great a shame to lose the ships that be lost'. It also stresses the need for escort ships, suggesting without them the supplies could be lost. This is reinforced by the word 'adventure,' suggesting in this context that masters could be gambling with the ships and supplies if they do not wait for escort vessels. The first source shows what can go wrong without adequate provisions while the second suggests Wolsey has thought of everything, and the third emphasises the dangers attendant on them crossing the Channel.

In conclusion, then we could argue that while all three sources show the importance of adequate supplies and Sources 1 and 3 focus on potential problems, Source 2 shows the extent of the provisions and in so doing suggests the problems may be surmounted by careful preparation and logistics.

Useful summary of the points made so far, reminding the examiner that the question focus has been maintained.

Uses language to comment on tone of source.

20/20
The candidate has analysed the sources comparatively in terms of how far they agree on the problems of provision.
There are useful examples in support of points made.
The conclusion is finely drawn from the comments made.
There is a very tight focus on the question.

Section 1: Henry VIII and the quest for international influence

b) Do you agree with the view that Scotland remained a threat to England between the years 1509–1540? Explain your answer using Sources 4, 5 and 6 and your own knowledge.

Bringing in own knowledge from the outset.

Shows how two of the sources disagree.

Relates the introduction to the question focus.

Scotland was a traditional ally of France and so whenever England was at war with France, there was the fear of war on two fronts. If an English army invaded France there was always the fear that the north of England may be undefended from a Scottish attack. Henry VII had tried to minimise this risk by marrying his daughter Margaret to the Scottish King, James IV, but the threat still remained. Moreover, both sides frequently raided along the border areas. In one of his attempts to make peace with France, Henry VIII wrote to the French king, 'Beware lest the affairs of Scotland should damage our friendship.' Having said this, Sources 4 and 5 disagree that Scotland was a threat throughout the period 1509–47 because Source 5 suggests Scotland was no longer a threat after the emphatic defeat at Flodden in 1513, while Source 4 suggests the threat continued. Thomas Cromwell believed the threat was so real that he advocated England taking Scotland over completely. He felt England could never be secure while Scotland was independent.

Integration of sources into candidate's knowledge.

When Henry led his army to France in 1513 he appointed the Earl of Surrey to defend the North in the event of Scottish attack. James indeed took advantage of the absence of the English army to invade England. Surrey had however deployed his own forces very effectively, with three lines of defence, one led by him in the North, a second in the Midlands led by Sir Thomas Lovell and a third in the South marshalled by Queen Catherine, who was acting as regent. On 9 September 1513, the Scots were defeated at Flodden, with King James and many of his nobles killed. This was a devastating blow; he left a baby child as king and his wife, Henry's sister, became regent. This effectively gave Henry considerable authority in Scotland and led Source 5 to argue that the Scots no longer posed a threat. It says they were demoralised and in no position to attack England again. Source 4 disagrees however. It argues that the Scots remained a threat particularly when England was at war with France because Scotland was France's traditional ally. Also they could be seeking revenge, and could not have resisted the temptation to invade when English troops were occupied on the continent. In Source 6, Cromwell in fact felt so strongly about this that he advised Henry to invade and absorb Scotland.

Discusses reliability of Source 6.

However, Source 6 is a speech to Parliament by a backbench MP. It would be in his interests to emphasise the threat, and we do not know if he was actually saying what he thought Henry wanted to hear or simply voicing his own opinion. Cromwell appeared to be worrying that we would be less likely to subdue France, and advocated attacking Scotland instead. Scotland would be easier to conquer because it had a land border with England, through which England could invade; 'it is but a simpleness for us to think to keep possessions in France, which is severed from us by the ocean sea and suffer Scotland, joined unto us by nature in all one island, unto which we may have recourse at all times when we will, which also to subdue'. Clearly England had to prepare itself for the ongoing threat of Scotland even if Scotland wasn't posing a specific threat at the time.

As Source 4 emphasises, this threat became more real when Margaret was overthrown as regent and the Duke of Albany took her place. Albany indeed was pro-French and sought to renew the alliance with France. Scarisbrick argues that it was partly to prevent this that Wolsey sought an alliance with France in 1518. It is in this context that Cromwell made his 1523 speech. However, Henry's policy was less ambitious. He made the offer of a fifteen-year truce with the Scots if they would get rid of Albany. When this was rejected, English troops raided the border areas. An uneasy peace was maintained until James V was ready to rule France himself and took a succession of French wives.

While there was no war between England and Scotland until the closing years of Henry's reign, Source 5 may be overstepping the mark to say that Scotland posed no threat, while Source 4 may have been more convincing if it had emphasised the ongoing threat of Scotland rather than specific instances which didn't develop into conflict. Cromwell, in Source 6, was a relatively unknown MP when he made his speech in 1523; he may have made it to get noticed. He recognised that English conquest of Scotland would be a blow to the French but it is difficult to judge how influential his speech was.

We can conclude that Scotland always posed a threat because of its alliance with France, and England had to be prepared to meet that threat should it ever materialise. However, Scotland was in too much disorder during most of the period to pose a specific threat. After having been soundly beaten at Flodden and its king having been killed, his child succeeded him and a regent ruled Scotland for most of the period until 1540. Source 4 recognises that the potential threat was evident but gives little evidence in the extract of specific examples. Source 5 is perhaps too dismissive. In Source 6, Cromwell may have had little influence in 1523 and was suggesting England should invade Scotland instead of attacking France, which was more risky. In all cases England did see Scotland as a potential, if not always actual, enemy.

Brings in another historian's view.

Critical engagement with the sources.

Conclusion comes to a judgement based on question focus, using knowledge and sources.

35/40
This is a very good essay. It integrates the sources with the candidate's own knowledge and the focus on the question is maintained throughout. For full marks, the essay could have started with a clearer statement of its argument in the introduction and there could have been more cross-referencing earlier in the essay.

Reverse engineering

The best essays are based on careful plans. Read the essay and the examiner's comments and try to work out the general points of the plan used to write the essay. Once you have done this, note down the specific examples used to support each general point.

Section 2: Structure of government

The rise of Thomas Wolsey

Thomas Wolsey was significant both as a churchman and statesman. He came to dominate government during the first twenty years of Henry's reign until his fall from power in 1529.

Wolsey's background

Wolsey was born in Ipswich in about 1475, the son of a prosperous butcher. As a clever child who wanted to rise above his parents' station in life, the only career open to him was the Church. In 1497 he was ordained a priest. Later he became Chaplain to Henry VII, who trusted him enough to send him on various diplomatic missions, where he developed contacts abroad.

In 1509, Wolsey became **Royal Almoner** to Henry VIII, responsible for organising charitable giving. He attached himself to the King, who began to regard him as a 'fixer'. Wolsey felt the King should have just one major advisor – himself.

Wolsey had very useful skills:

- He was a brilliant organiser. He organised, for example, the supplies and equipment for Henry's war against France in 1513.
- He had an excellent eye for detail. Little escaped him.
- He was witty, cultured and excellent company – far from a dry administrator.

Henry came to depend on Wolsey not only because he trusted his advice, but because Wolsey took the burden of administration. Henry found office work tedious. He was prepared to delegate it to those he trusted. However if he lost his trust in them, he could be ruthless.

Church preferment

Wolsey was primarily a churchman who happened also to be a statesman. He attained very high honours in the Church.

- After the successful French war in 1513 he was rewarded for his services by being made Bishop of the captured town of Tournai. He later sold the bishopric back to the French for 12,000 **livres**.
- In 1514 he was also made Archbishop of York after the death of the incumbent, Archbishop Bainbridge in Rome.
- In 1515 he was made a Cardinal.
- In 1518 he became a **Papal legate,** effectively the Head of the Church in England with the authority to remit sins, demand tribute from church leaders such as bishops, and criticise clergy. This was in addition to appointing others to church offices, reforming monasteries and absolving those **excommunicated**.

Role in government

Wolsey also attained high offices in government:

- In 1515, Henry retired two of his most senior ministers, William Warham as **Lord Chancellor** and Bishop Fox as **Lord Privy Seal**. Both had served his father.
- In 1515, Wolsey became Lord Chancellor and his supporter Thomas Rothall became Lord Privy Seal.
- Both of these offices controlled the seals that authenticated royal orders. Wolsey was then the second most powerful personage in the kingdom.
- As Lord Chancellor, Wolsey was effectively head of the Government. He was the King's chief advisor and controlled considerable patronage. Among other duties, Wolsey prepared abstracts of important letters for the King, and dealt with the day to day detail of governance for which Henry had little patience.

Support or challenge? (a)

Below is a sample exam-style part (a) question which asks how far the sources agree with a specific statement. Below this are a series of sources. Decide whether the sources support or challenge the statement in the question.

> How far do Sources 1, 2 and 3 agree that Henry VIII made Thomas Wolsey his chief minister due to his organisational skills? Explain your answer, using the evidence of Sources 1, 2 and 3.

	SUPPORT	CHALLENGE
Source 1		
Source 2		
Source 3		

SOURCE 1

(From J J Scarisbrick, *Henry VIII*, published 1968)

There is no doubt that at times Henry was furiously involved in public business and in commanding partnership with Wolsey, and that he could break into his minister's conduct of affairs with decisive results. There is no doubt that he had intense interest in certain things – in ships, in war, in what Francis I was doing for example.

SOURCE 2

(From Nancy Lenz Harvey, *Thomas Cardinal Wolsey*, published 1980)

Wolsey knew himself to be able. He knew his vision, his political vision, keen and more comprehensive than those who sought petty goals and private motive. He knew he shared with Henry a quality of mind far superior to those about them. Henry for his part knew the value of industry born of ability. Like his father before him, the King cared far less for bloodlines than he did the quality of service.

SOURCE 3

(Richard Fox, Bishop of Winchester, writing to Wolsey)

… I had never better will to serve the king … And specially since your good lordship hath the great charge that ye have in your hand: perceiving better, straighter and speedier ways of justice and more diligence and labour for the king's rights, duties and profits to be in you than ever I see in time past in any other.

Mind map

Use the information on the opposite page and your own knowledge to add detail to a copy of the mind map below to show how the different aspects helped Wolsey in his rise to power.

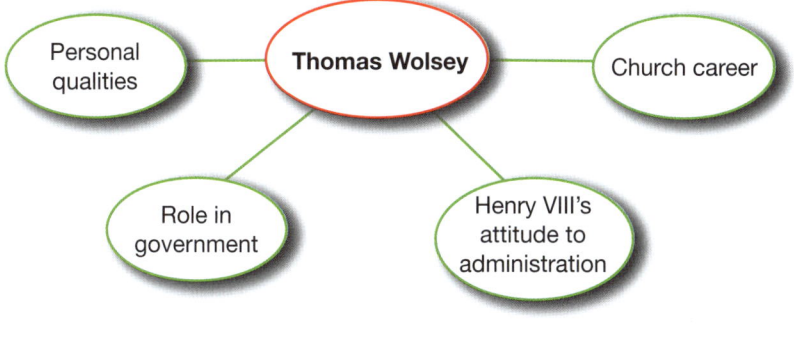

Section 2: Structure of government

Wolsey as Cardinal and Papal Legate

Wolsey became the most powerful churchman at a time when anti-clericalism was growing in England. As Cardinal and Papal legate, Wolsey had the power to determine the direction of the Church in England.

Anti-Clericalism

There was criticism of various types of corruption such as **pluralcies**, where clergymen had more than one parish, where priests kept mistresses or had illegitimate children and where fees were charged for services such as burials.

- Many people wanted to read the Bible in English but were unable to do so.
- It was felt that the church courts were unfair, where clergymen would receive light sentences and lay people could be tried for heresy without a fair hearing. This came into focus in the case of Richard Hunne in 1511.
- Richard Hunne was a wealthy London merchant in dispute with his parish priest. The Bishop of London intervened to have Hunne arrested for heresy. In prison, Hunne was found hanged. When the Bishop's Chancellor was accused of murder, the Bishop appealed to Wolsey and the whole affair was hushed up. This led to growing criticism of senior churchmen.

This came at a time when the **Renaissance** questioned many beliefs, and the invention of printing made new ideas spread more easily. In 1519, Luther wrote his **Ninety-Five Theses** and sparked off the **Reformation** across central Europe. While England appeared loyal to Rome, questions were asked about the conduct of the Church.

As Papal legate, Wolsey did little to reform the Church:

- He appeared relatively untroubled by corruption. He himself had two illegitimate children for whom he found careers in the Church.
- He never visited any of the cathedrals over which he was Bishop until the end of his career, when he went to York.
- He weakened the morale of the bishops because as legate he superseded their authority.
- He often kept bishoprics vacant or appointed foreigners who never visited, so he could take the revenues himself.
- He was quite lax on the spread of new ideas. **Lutheran** ideas spread unchecked at Cardinal College, Oxford, which he had founded.

> As Head of the Church in England, Wolsey's failings and unpopularity added to anti-clericalism. With his extravagant lifestyle and laxity, he was increasingly seen as personifying all that was wrong with the Church.

Wolsey did suppress some monasteries in order to finance the building of Cardinal Colleges in Oxford and his hometown of Ipswich. In total, 29 monasteries were suppressed. There were precedents for this. Bishop Fisher of Rochester had suppressed two in 1524 to finance the building of St John's College, Cambridge. Perhaps as a sign of what was to follow in the following decade, Thomas Cromwell was his main agent in the suppressions, and they led to unrest and riots, for example in Bayham, Surrey.

Wolsey did little for the Church he led and it was his failure to persuade the Pope to agree to a divorce that was instrumental in his downfall.

Identify an argument

Below are a series of definitions, a sample exam-style part (b) question and two sample conclusions. One of the conclusions achieves a high level because it contains an argument. The other achieves a lower level because it contains only description and assertion. Identify which is which. The mark scheme on pages 4–5 will help you.

- **Description:** a detailed account.
- **Assertion:** a statement of fact or an opinion, which is not supported by reason.
- **Reason:** a statement that explains or justifies something.
- **Argument:** an assertion justified with a reason.

Do you agree that the Church was corrupt and in need of reform in the 1520s? Explain your answer using Sources 1, 2 and 3 and your own knowledge.

Sample 1

> There was a lot of corruption and abuse in the Church in the 1520s. Many clergymen had more than one parish, and some were even married with children. Wolsey himself had a son, for whom he found a cushy job in the Church. There was a tunnel between one monastery and a nunnery. Clergymen charged high fees for services such as burials. In the church courts clergymen would receive light sentences and lay people could be tried for heresy without a fair hearing.

Sample 2

> Source 2 suggests that Wolsey saw the need to reform the Church in England, even though Source 1 shows he shared in its corrupt practices himself. Source 3 adds that Wolsey was flashy in his clothes, not at all like a clergyman should be, for example. Many people felt that the Church needed reform in the 1520s. They suggested, as we can see in Source 1, that there was wholesale abuse, such as priests only being appointed because they knew the patron, having more than one parish and charging high fees for services such as burials which people had no choice but to pay. While the Church undoubtedly did much good through charitable work and education, there was widespread evidence of abuse, particularly in the higher echelons. Wolsey for example lived very extravagantly and did nothing to reform the Church despite the intentions laid out in Source 2. In fact if Wolsey's extravagance as identified in Source 3 led to his deep unpopularity among the clergy he would find it difficult to lead them in reforms. At a time when printing made new ideas more readily available, calls for reform were becoming more vocal.

SOURCE 1
(From David H Pill, The English Reformation, *published 1973)*

Sometimes livings were filled with people with no other qualifications than kinship with the patron. Some were held by members of the same family for generations. Thomas Wolsey … made careful provision for the future of his son Thomas Wynter. He was Dean of Wells while he was still a schoolboy, and as the years went by, further preferments were provided until his income from the Church came to £2,700 a year. His father kept most of this though, making him an allowance of £200.

SOURCE 2
(From Nancy Lenz Harvey, Thomas Cardinal Wolsey, *published 1980)*

[Wolsey] would have the clergy deliver 'plain preaching to the people in the vulgar tongue (English).' He would insist on precise instruction of both clergy and congregation in the articles of faith; he would persevere in the necessity of the administering of all the sacraments, in the collection of tithes and offerings; he would hold all archdeacons and priests to the fulfilment of sacred duty. He would check the abuses of the clergy; he would chastise those who lapsed into Lutheran musings. He would reform Holy Church in England.

SOURCE 3
(From Polydore Vergil, History of England, *published in 1555)*

As far as I am aware, he was both the first and the last of the entire priesthood, including bishops and Cardinals, to wear an outer garment made of silk, also rashly adopted by those priests who wished to curry his favour. And indeed this mannerism, silly as it was, created great hostility among the priesthood caste.

27

Section 2: Structure of government

Wolsey as Lord Chancellor – the government of England 1509–29

Henry VII had controlled the administration personally, but his son preferred to leave the job to trusted civil servants, many of whom had served his father, for example, Sir John Heron, who was Treasurer of the Chamber from 1492 to 1521. However, Wolsey came to dominate the Government from 1515, when he was appointed Lord Chancellor.

- In 1512, a fire had burnt down the old Palace at Westminster, where the king traditionally resided.
- Henry became more nomadic, his court moving between palaces such as Greenwich and Eltham on the fringes of London.
- Wolsey remained firmly in London, at the centre of the Government.
- Wolsey changed the role of the **King's Council**, whose members traditionally advised the king, and also sat in the **Court of the Star Chamber**, administering justice.
- Wolsey developed the role of the Star Chamber in terms of upholding the law. This meant its members were too busy to give advice to the King, who was rarely in London.
- Wolsey increasingly took this role on himself, and reported to the Councillors when executive decisions had already been made.

Keeping close to the King

Wolsey knew that he owed his position to the King, and needed to keep in close contact with him to maintain it.

- He had been advised by Richard Fox, Bishop of Winchester to 'keep close to the King'. He sent messengers to the King every day and had his own weekly audience. However, as the court moved around, this wasn't always possible.
- In 1517, at the time of a sweating sickness epidemic, Wolsey fell ill and missed regular contacts.
- The King moved around frequently and in one year only met with his Lord Chancellor once from July to the end of the year.
- To see the King, people increasingly had to go through Wolsey. Henry was not happy about this and frequently complained that he was denuded of learned advice.

The Eltham Ordinances, 1526

In 1526, the **Eltham Ordinances** attempted to address the issue of providing the King with a team of advisors. As well as checks on court expenditure and limits on the numbers of people entitled to free board and lodging, these laid down that Henry should always have twenty leading Councillors at his beck and call. However, Wolsey said all major office holders should work in London. Given that the King's Court moved around, this meant in effect that Henry never had more than four Councillors around him. While the King wanted the presence of trusted Councillors, Wolsey wanted them absent.

It was after the Eltham Ordinances that the King began to lose confidence in Wolsey, and frequently he went behind his back, particularly over efforts to get his marriage to Catherine of Aragon annulled. After Wolsey's fall from power, Henry acquired Wolsey's residence of York House in Westminster. He was now at the centre again, and the Council then began to attend to him personally. Henry had regained power himself.

Wolsey had strengthened royal power by acting as Henry's chief advisor, centralising authority and neutralising rivals – giving Henry an exemplar to follow.

28

Add own knowledge

Below are a sample exam-style part (b) question and the three sources referred to in the question. In one colour, draw links between the sources to show ways in which they agree about the significance of Wolsey's personal influence in government. In another colour, draw links between the sources to show ways in which they disagree. Around the edge of the sources, write relevant own knowledge. Again, draw links to show the ways this agrees and disagrees with the sources.

> Do you agree with the view that Wolsey reformed the royal household to increase his own personal influence? Explain your answer using Sources 1, 2 and 3 and your own knowledge.

SOURCE 1

(From D Starkey, Privy Secrets: Henry VIII and the Lords of the Council, *published 1987)*

[Wolsey turned to the task of the 'reformation' of the royal household.]

The result was the publication of the Ordinances of Eltham in July 1526. The Household (save for its accounting machinery) and the Chamber were passed over cursorily; for the Privy Chamber on the other hand, detailed regulations were prescribed and a full listing of its personnel given. Next came the chapters dealing with the Council. Their ostensible purpose was to provide for 'a good number' of councillors to give 'their attendance on the King's most royal person'.

SOURCE 2

(From Nancy Lenz Harvey, Cardinal Thomas Wolsey, *published 1980)*

He drew up the Ordinances of Eltham against 'the great confusion, annoyance, infection, trouble and dishonour, that ensueth by the numbers as well of sickly, impotent, inable and unmet persons,' as of 'rascals and vagabonds in all the court'. Gentlemen ushers were moved to vigilance to end wholesale theft. The knight harbinger was required 'to banish lewd women from the Household'.

SOURCE 3

(From Polydore Vergil, History of England, *published in 1555)*

Wolsey carried on all the business at his own will since no one was of more value to the King. Thus by his insolence and ambition Wolsey sought and earned the dislike of the entire people, since he was hated by Peerage and Commons alike, because they were very indignant at his vainglory. He was a universal loathing of hate because he imagined he could undertake any responsibility at all. And it was a sight worth seeing to see this man, ignorant of the law, sitting on the bench and pronouncing justice …

And so Wolsey's administration originally had a shadow of justice in public esteem, but because it was a shadow it quickly disappeared, as Wolsey began doing everything according to his own whim, since nobody enjoyed more favour with the King.

Section 2: Structure of government

Relations with nobility and Parliament

The period following 1515 saw Wolsey lose some of his influence with the King, to be replaced by that of the Privy Council. However, this was a gradual development. Wolsey's problem concerning regular access to Henry was always a weakness with his system. He was based in Westminster and Henry's court moved around. Even though he held regular meetings and there were daily couriers, this remained a concern, not least because Henry was surrounded by courtiers who were also ready to offer advice — and displace Wolsey if they could.

Most nobles hated Wolsey because of his low social origins. Henry supported him for this very reason. Wolsey owed everything to Henry's continued support. Henry didn't want to see the nobility become too powerful because of the turmoil of the Wars of the Roses of the previous century, when powerful nobles had fought for control of a weak king, and the still uncertain position of his own dynasty. In this sense, Wolsey was a useful foil. He could take the blame for unpopular policies.

Affair of the 'minions'

Henry increasingly began to be surrounded by men like himself — young, adventurous, incautious. They were known as 'the minions'. Notable among these was the Duke of Suffolk, his most trusted friend. They formed the Privy Council. Worried by their influence, Wolsey introduced Richard Pace and Sir Thomas More to court. Both reported to Wolsey. Pace became secretary to Henry, while More was Councillor-attendant, acting as liaison between Wolsey and the King.

In May 1519, Wolsey managed to get the minions expelled from court on the grounds that they gave Henry bad advice. They were replaced by four courtiers who acted as body servants and councillors — again, Wolsey's men. Henry was concerned about the amount of influence that Wolsey had, and after the Eltham Ordinances, began to trust him less. The later 1520s saw the growth in influence of the Privy Council.

The Privy Council

This was a Council made up of people who attended on the King. In this respect, its members had far more regular access to the King than Wolsey. By 1540, the Privy Council had become the most important organisation in the Tudor Government. Its growth in power and influence can be plotted from the 1520s onward. By the late 1520s, it was dominated by the **Boleyn faction**, who hated Wolsey because they felt he was delaying the annulment Henry sought from Catherine of Aragon. They accused Wolsey of subverting conciliar government by dominating access to the King. In 1529, Parliament recognised the Council as third in the governmental hierarchy, below the offices of Chancellor and Treasurer.

It is important to note however that Wolsey was now trusted less by Henry, and his time was increasingly dominated by the divorce — giving members of the Privy Council more influence. They may have moved sooner against Wolsey, but most of them had no more liking for the tedious work of bureaucracy than the King himself.

RAG – Rate the timeline

Below are a question and a timeline. Read the question, study the timeline and, using three coloured pens, put a red, amber or green star next to the events to show:

- **Red:** Events and policies that have no relevance to the question
- **Amber:** Events and policies that have some relevance to the question
- **Green:** Events and policies that are directly relevant to the question

How far do you agree that Thomas Wolsey was more concerned with reforming the Government than the Church in the years 1512 to 1529? Explain your answer using your own knowledge.

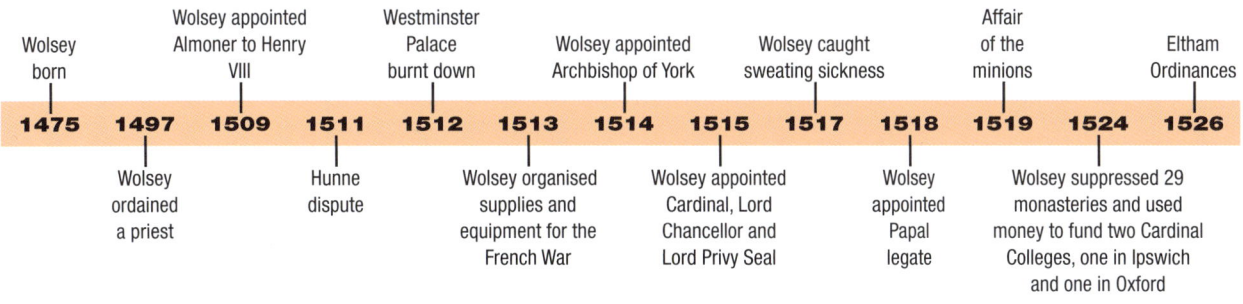

Write the question

The following sources relate to the influence of Thomas Wolsey on the governance of England. Read the information on the page opposite about Wolsey's role in governing England. Having done this, write two exam-style part (b) questions using the sources.

SOURCE 1

(From D Wilson, A Brief History of Henry VIII, *published 2009)*

He had the whole council [and Queen Catherine] behind him in protesting about the antics of the minions ... By the time the minions returned in summer of 1519, the staff of the Privy Chamber had been augmented by four older men who were also members of the Council. This sequence of events provides yet another example of the standing of personal relationships to any understanding of Henry VIII and his policies. Great events could and sometimes did depend on an idea spoken or a joke shared in the intimate confines of the Privy Chamber.

SOURCE 2

(From D Starkey, Privy Secrets: Henry VIII and his Council, *published 1987)*

In autumn 1518 [the minions] consolidated their position at court by acquiring the formal office of gentlemen of the Privy Chamber; eight months later in May 1519, Wolsey procured their expulsion from court on the grounds that they were a bad influence on the King. In their place he put four 'men of greater age, and perhaps of greater repute, but creatures of Cardinal Wolsey'.

SOURCE 3

(From a letter by Guistinian, Venetian Ambassador, 1518)

[Wolsey] is about forty-six, very handsome, learned, extremely eloquent, of vast ability and indefatigable. He alone transacts the same business as that which occupies all the magistracies, offices, and councils of Venice, both civilian and criminal; all state affairs.

Section 2: Structure of government

Wolsey, Parliament and attempts to raise revenue

Wolsey needed Parliament to raise revenues for the King. If it were not for the costs of the wars, he may have attempted to govern without it. When taxes were required, Parliament had to agree a subsidy, and then Commissioners would collect it. Parliament met in 1523 for the first time in eight years. Wolsey, like the King, expected its members to agree to taxes out of patriotism and loyalty. Clearly however, people were unhappy about paying taxes. Tax commissioners had found it difficult to raise the revenue expected in 1513, and indeed didn't complete their task until 1515. Even then, Henry accepted pleas of poverty from nineteen towns and let them off paying.

> In 1523, in attempting to raise a subsidy of £800,000, Wolsey was told by Parliament to moderate his demands. He was told such a sum would bankrupt the country. After four years, only £151,215 had been collected. This was the first graduated tax, with those on incomes of over £20 paying proportionally more than those on £2. Below this, no payment was expected.

It was, however, the Amicable Grant of 1525 that effectively led to crisis, and showed the Henry wouldn't hesitate to make Wolsey a scapegoat if his own popularity was threatened.

The Amicable Grant, 1525

This was a levy of one-sixth of the goods of citizens and one-third on those of the clergy. Many places refused to pay altogether, while others offered goods instead of money.

Excuses included:

- lack of enthusiasm for the French wars they were expected to finance
- anti-clericalism
- unpopularity of Wolsey.

In the face of such reluctance, Wolsey told a meeting of London councillors that he would only collect from them what they could afford. News of this caused considerable resentment elsewhere, and in East Anglia passive resistance. Collection was suspended until the King was consulted. Henry was afraid of rebellion so he abandoned the Grant, blaming Wolsey and saying he hadn't been told about it. Wolsey got the blame, while in fact some historians think it was Wolsey who had in fact persuaded the King to abandon it.

Nevertheless, Henry learnt much from this episode:

- He needed the support of taxpayers.
- He couldn't risk rebellion in the south-east, not only because people in the south-east tended to be his most loyal supporters but also because it was too near to his own places of residence for comfort.

He was also afraid that the serious uprisings in Germany might spread to England.

In fact, people didn't object to taxation if they agreed with its purpose. Henry became more wary about funding war or his allies, and the revenues collected began more to reflect the interests of the taxpayers – notably on defence rather on aggression. Where there was resistance, it was always localised and mainly based on poverty.

Mind map

Use the information on the opposite page and your own knowledge to add detail to a copy of the mind map below to show how and why taxation was collected in the first twenty years of Henry's reign.

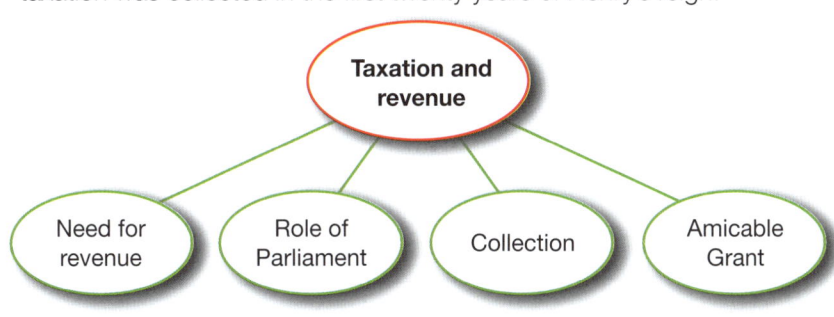

Doing reliability well

Below are a series of definitions listing common reasons why sources can be unreliable, a sample exam-style part (a) question and a series of sources. Under each source explain why the source is either reliable or unreliable for the purpose stated, justifying your answer by referring to the following definitions.

- **Vested interest:** the source is written so that the writer can protect their power or their own interests.
- **Second-hand report:** the writer of the source is not an eyewitness, but is relying on someone else's account.
- **Expertise:** the source is written on a subject which the author (for example a historian) is an expert.
- **Political bias:** a source is written by a politician and it reflects their political views.
- **Reputation:** a source is written to protect the writer's reputation.

How far do Sources 1, 2 and 3 agree that there was considerable opposition to the attempt to raise taxes in the 1520s? Explain your answer using the evidence of Sources 1, 2 and 3.

SOURCE 1

(Speech by Cardinal Wolsey to Parliament in 1523)

And whereas for the furniture of the said war, both defensive and offensive, ye have, after long pain, travail, great charges and costs, devised, made and offered an honourable and right large subsidy, which ye now have presented, in the name and behalf of all subjects, unto his majesty, his grace doth not only right acceptably and thankfully receive, admit and take the same, but also therefore giveth unto you his most hearty thanks, assuring the same that his grace shall in such wise employ the said subsidy and loving contribution, as shall be to the defence of his realm, and of you, his subjects and the persecution and pressing of his enemy.

Source 1 is reliable/unreliable as evidence about the opposition against raising taxes in the 1520s because _____

SOURCE 2

(Report by the Duke of Norfolk from Lavenham on those gathered to protest about the Amicable Grant, 1525)

They came all in their shirts and kneeling before us with piteous crying for pity showed that they were the King's most humble and faithful subjects and so would continue during their lives saying this offence by them committed was only for lack of work so that they knew not how to get their living.

Source 2 is reliable/unreliable as evidence about the opposition against raising taxes in the 1520s because _____

SOURCE 3

(From A Fletcher, Tudor Rebellions*, published in 1968. He is writing about reactions to the Amicable Grant)*

There had been some resistance to the 1523 subsidy in Yorkshire where the commons of Craven and Richmondshire had proved recalcitrant; the south-east, however, had paid in full. But the attitude to the new **extra Parliamentary grant** was from the first sullen and unwilling.

Source 3 is reliable/unreliable as evidence about the opposition against raising taxes in the 1520s because _____

Section 2: Structure of government

The fall of Wolsey 1529–30

The fall of Wolsey was sudden and related to his failure to achieve the annulment of Henry's marriage to Catherine of Aragon (see page 42).

Despite his power and authority, Wolsey knew he needed the support of the King to survive. Wolsey had made many enemies. There were many general and specific groups who hated Wolsey, from nobles jealous of his power and status to taxpayers who blamed him for the costly wars against France. In addition, Henry had started to bypass Wolsey, particularly on matters of the divorce. For example, he sent William Knights to obtain a **Papal bull** to allow him to marry a woman to whom he was already related – to give him permission to marry Anne Boleyn after having had an affair with her sister.

Relations with the Boleyn faction

Nevertheless, Wolsey felt secure until 1529, when he appeared to lose the support of Anne Boleyn after the failure of the **Legatine Court**. Like the King, she had relied on Wolsey to obtain an annulment of the royal marriage. She had the ear of Henry, especially during the **Royal progress**, when the court was in constant attendance, and Wolsey met the King only irregularly. Even then, it became difficult to see Henry alone. On returning from a mission to France, Wolsey had to report to both Henry and Anne Boleyn.

Evidence suggests that the Boleyn faction had been plotting against Wolsey in July 1529, but Henry, still loyal to his Chancellor, forestalled them. In October, Wolsey's foreign policy aims came into conflict with Henry's, over whether to seek a French alliance. A meeting at Grafton, although cordial, failed to settle their differences. Again, Anne dragged Henry off to prevent further discussions. Henry withdrew his support for Wolsey, allowing the alliance of the Boleyn faction and nobles such as the Dukes of Norfolk and Suffolk to move against him. While the latter both sought high office, the Boleyn faction wanted to extend their influence through Anne becoming queen.

Wolsey's dismissal and death

Wolsey was accused of **praemunire**, against which he had no defence – he had used his powers as Papal legate to influence the Crown. He was dismissed as Lord Chancellor, and had his property confiscated by the King. However, he retained his Archbishopric at York and was still wealthy. As if to protect him from further accusations, Sir Thomas More, under the King's orders, made a speech in Parliament saying Wolsey has 'been gently corrected,' implying that now the affair was over.

In February 1530, Wolsey was pardoned. He had lost his political power, but was still powerful in the Church. Perhaps he should have been satisfied. His enemies still feared his return, and continued their machinations against him – including intercepting his letters.

Wolsey sought complete reinstatement by plotting with unfriendly powers, notably France, possibly to drag England into war with Charles V. However, his attempts were discovered and reported to the King. On his way to answer charges of high treason, Wolsey died at Leicester on 29 November 1530.

Spot the inference

High level answers avoid summarising or paraphrasing the sources, and instead make inferences from the sources. Below is a series of statements. Read Source 2 below and decide which of the statements:

- make inference from the source (I)
- paraphrase the source (P)
- summarise the source (S)
- cannot be justified from the source (X).

Statement	I	P	S	X
Henry relied on others for advice and support.				
Anne Boleyn's relatives realised they could use her influence with the King to bring about the fall of Wolsey.				
Wolsey was a habit that was difficult to break.				
Anne Boleyn could influence the King in his political decision making.				
Henry didn't rely on Anne Boleyn for political advice but her relatives realised they could use her as a bridgehead to influence him.				

Develop the detail

Below are a sample exam-style part (b) question and a paragraph written in answer to the question. The paragraph contains a limited amount of detail. Annotate the paragraph to add additional detail to the answer.

> Do you agree that the opposition of the King was the most important factor in the dismissal of Thomas Wolsey in 1529? Explain your answer using Sources 1 and 2 and your own knowledge.

Sources 1 and 2 imply that it was not the King who was Wolsey's main enemy. However, both sources agree that Wolsey had other powerful enemies who were seeking his destruction, including members of the nobility who envied his power, and taxpayers, who resented the taxes he imposed. Source 2 comes close to specifically identifying the Boleyn faction as being responsible. In this sense, Henry's opposition was not the most important factor in the dismissal of Wolsey because the plotting of the Boleyn faction prompted Henry to dismiss a minister he had once trusted.

SOURCE 1

(From J J Scarisbrick, Henry VIII, *published 1968)*

The truth seems to be that it was not Henry who was Wolsey's fiercest enemy and not he who wanted his complete bloody destruction. Henry was unable to forget either his failures or how remarkable a servant he had been and might be. But Wolsey was not restored. If Henry had momentarily faltered, Wolsey's enemies were quick to push the King onwards.

SOURCE 2

(From D Wilson, A Brief History of Henry VIII, *published 2009)*

Henry always needed others to lean on for advice and emotional support. For years Wolsey had been his main prop and stay. He had become a habit, not always wholesome but difficult to break. Now another had interposed herself between king and councillor. Henry did not rely on her for political advice but she could work on his prejudices and provide a bridgehead for her father, her brother, her uncle, the Duke of Norfolk and their allies who realised that they now had their best opportunity in years for removing the hated Cardinal.

Section 2: Structure of government

Section 2: Exam focus

On pages 37–39 are sample A-grade answers to the exam-style questions on these two pages. Read the answers and the examiner's comments around them.

a) How far does the evidence of Sources 1, 2 and 3 suggest that Wolsey's fall from power was complete following his dismissal in October 1529? Explain your answer, using the evidence of Sources 1, 2 and 3.

b) Do you agree with the view that the main reason Thomas Wolsey fell from power in October 1529 was because he had failed to get the King's marriage to Catherine of Aragon annulled? Explain your answer using Sources 4, 5 and 6 and your own knowledge.

SOURCE 1

(From Du Bellay, the French Ambassador to Montmercy, Constable of France, dated 17 October 1529)

I have visited the Cardinal in his troubles. He is the greatest example of misfortune that one could see. He represented his case to me in the worst rhetoric I ever saw; for heart and tongue failed him completely. He wept and prayed that Francis and Madame would have pity on him if they found that he had kept his promise to be a good servant to them as far as his honour would permit. But at last he left me without being able to say anything more to me than his countenance did, which has lost half its animation … He does not desire legateship, seal of office or influence, is ready to give up everything to his shirt and go and live in a hermitage if this King will not keep him in disfavour.

SOURCE 2

(From Chapuys, Imperial Ambassador to Charles V, dispatch dated 25 October 1529)

The downfall of the Cardinal is complete. He is dismissed from the council, deprived of the chancellorship and constrained to make an inventory of his goods in his own hand that nothing is forgotten. It is said he has acknowledged his faults and presented all his effects to the King … The King either moved by pity or for fear if he should die the whole extent of his effects would not be found, sent him a ring for comfort. People say execrable things of him, all of which be known at this Parliament. But those who raised the storm will not let it abate, not knowing if he returns to power what would become of them.

SOURCE 3

(From E W Ives, The Fall of Wolsey, *1991)*

What his enemies still wanted, of course, was security against a Wolsey come-back action to make certain that 'he be so provided for that he never have any power hereafter to trouble', perhaps as was claimed; 'the commonwealth,' but most certainly themselves.

SOURCE 4

(From Polydore Vergil, History of England, *published in 1555)*

Oh, the human condition, so uncertain at birth and weak during life! Wolsey was abounding in dignity and wealth when he undertook the business of the King's marriage, which he fancied would bring him happiness, but it was his downfall.

SOURCE 5

(From D Wilson, A Brief History of Henry VIII, *published 2009)*

[Wolsey] was the Government and since it is every Englishman's birthright to be against the Government, every Englishman – or so it seemed – was against Wolsey. He was blamed for all the ills that had befallen the realm. Catherine's supporters accused him of beginning the annulment issues. Henry's friends believed that he was trying to thwart the annulment. Radicals condemned him for persecuting suspected heretics. Reactionary churchmen resented his softly-softly approach to heterodoxy. Taxpayers held the Cardinal responsible for England's involvement in costly wars with France and merchants grumbled about the effects on trade of his anti-imperial policies.

SOURCE 6

(From R Hutchinson, Thomas Cromwell, *published 2006)*

The blow may have been expected by some, but nevertheless when it struck, the shock and awe were felt across all England. Cardinal Thomas Wolsey, prince of the Church, European statesman and Henry VIII's Lord Chancellor had fallen from power. His **nemesis** was Anne Boleyn, whom he described privately as the King's own 'night crow'.

a) How far does the evidence of Sources 1, 2 and 3 suggest that Wolsey's fall from power was complete following his dismissal in October 1529? Explain your answer, using the evidence of Sources 1, 2 and 3.

Cross-references all 3 sources to address question.

Sources 1 and 2 seem to agree that Wolsey's power was completely broken by his dismissal. Source 1 suggests he was broken in mind and body, weeping and unable to get his words out, while Source 2 suggests he has given up all his offices. However Source 3, written perhaps with the benefit of hindsight, suggests that his enemies still feared him and were afraid he would make a comeback. This would threaten their own positions although they couched their concerns in the harm he would do to the country as a whole. This is in part borne out by the second source, which suggests that those who plotted Wolsey's downfall were afraid in case he returned to power.

Addresses provenance.

Sources 1 and 2 were both written by foreign ambassadors. Both may be saying what their monarchs wanted to hear. Source 1 suggests Wolsey is appealing to Francis for help because he has always favoured France; clearly this would flatter King Francis. It suggests Wolsey is ready to give up everything if only the King would restore his favour. Source 2 suggests he hasn't quite given up and could still be dangerous. This is in effect a warning that Wolsey could return to power because he was traditionally friendlier to France than to Spain. Source 2 also indicates that the King may feel pity for Wolsey — although his compassion could be because he doesn't want Wolsey to die before he has completed the inventory of his goods.

Challenges Source 1 in terms what is said in Source 2.

Makes inferences.

Nevertheless, Chapuys clearly feels the possibility of a comeback is real and great play is made that the King gave Wolsey a ring, which was a significant token. Clearly the Boleyn faction wouldn't feel secure until Wolsey was no longer a threat. The fact that they continued plotting suggests that they felt he could make a comeback. The Ambassadors' accounts both come from October, when Wolsey's dismissal was still news and they didn't know how it would develop. Indeed, their tone is one of surprise — Chapuys in Source 2 for example says Wolsey's downfall is complete as though this was a surprise. Du Bellay in Source 1 describes Wolsey's reaction if he were a broken man yet hoping for restitution, where he says if only he can regain the King's favour he would be happy to be a hermit — as if the support of the King is all that matters to him.

Uses sources to address question focus.

On the surface, the sources suggest Wolsey is indeed broken by his downfall, but two suggest he could make a comeback and these show that if this were the case he could still be a threat to his enemies. However, these are from foreign ambassadors who have their own agendas, seeing Wolsey's possible comeback in terms of how far it would benefit their own countries. Source 1 suggests that Wolsey could return through the help of the French King, because Wolsey had always been partial in his foreign policy towards France. Source 2 recognises the comeback would weaken the English court because he would be seeking revenge. This is corroborated in Source 3. Only the first source suggests he would retire if restored to favour. Therefore, according to these sources in total, Wolsey may have been down — but he wasn't out yet.

17/20

This is a very good source analysis, cross-referencing the sources and maintaining question focus, while also using the sources to challenge each other. There are some useful inferences, for example over the use of the ring. Provenance and attributes of each source are also addressed. A slightly stronger conclusion, which fully explains why Wolsey was down, but not out, would get full marks.

Section 2: Structure of government

b) Do you agree with the view that the main reason Thomas Wolsey fell from power in October 1529 was because he had failed to get the King's marriage to Catherine of Aragon annulled? Explain your answer using Sources 4, 5 and 6 and your own knowledge.

Cross-references the sources to address the question.

On the surface, Wolsey fell from power because he failed to get the King's marriage to Catherine of Aragon annulled. Sources 4 and 6 would appear to agree with this statement, with the latter overtly making the statement that Anne Boleyn was his downfall. However, Source 5 shows all the other reasons why Wolsey was unpopular. Henry had already distanced himself from Wolsey over the failure of the Amicable Grant in 1525, and there is evidence that he was losing confidence in his Chancellor. Wolsey always knew that he only survived through the support of the King and so it is likely that when he had lost the King's support, his dismissal would only be a matter of time.

Background knowledge.

Source 6 suggests that Anne Boleyn was primarily responsible for the fall of Wolsey, while Source 4 asserts it was the failure to arrange the divorce that had brought his downfall. Both these sources indicate that the reasons for Wolsey's fall lay at the centre of court. Wolsey's weak spot had always been access to the King. Anne Boleyn clearly had more regular access and could therefore criticise Wolsey to Henry when he wasn't there to defend himself. Access to the King was always a weakness in Wolsey's system of government. The Royal court moved around, while his base was London. Courtiers always had more access to the King than Wolsey and they undoubtedly used this access to blacken his name. However, while he was useful to Henry, he could be assured of his support. In the Affair of the Minions in 1519, for example, Henry had agreed to their temporarily being removed from court. Nobles such as the Dukes of Norfolk and Suffolk hated Wolsey, not only because of his power and influence over the King but also because he was a commoner. This was a main reason why Henry kept him in office – because he knew Wolsey owed his position to him and also he could be useful as someone to blame when things didn't go well, as in the Amicable Grant of 1525. In this sense, Source 5 is correct to list all the groups who sought his downfall. However, the fact that they sought his downfall didn't mean they would be successful.

Use of relevant examples.

Sources 4 and 6 both agree that the main reason was his inability to obtain the annulment desired by the King. Source 6 implies Wolsey didn't like Anne Boleyn, calling her a 'night crow.' Source 4 implies Wolsey was responsible in part for his own downfall because it was he who first suggested to the King the possibility of a divorce. He would have done this to remain in favour, because the King was increasingly concerned that Catherine might be beyond child-bearing age. However, Wolsey had nothing, as far as we know, to do with the King falling in love with Anne Boleyn. Nevertheless, she lost confidence in and patience with Wolsey, sometime in autumn 1529. The timing was significant, because it was when the court was on its Progress and so Wolsey wasn't in regular communication with Henry. He was, however, surrounded by 'the Boleyn faction' whom he had promoted to high positions. Anne's father for example had been made Lord Privy Seal, while the Duke of Norfolk was her uncle.

Analysis supported by accurate and relevant factual material.

Source 6 suggests that while some may have expected Wolsey's demise it did nevertheless come as a great surprise to many — the author mentions 'shock and awe'. This view may be supported by the fact that the Boleyn faction had been plotting against Wolsey for months. Henry apparently warned them against this — although there is evidence that Wolsey bought himself out of trouble by paying Thomas Boleyn some of the revenues from his Churchly incomes.

The question of access loomed again when Wolsey met Henry at Grafton. Apparently their negotiations were going well, but Anne distracted Henry so Wolsey left without agreement. Again this would suggest, as Sources 4 and 6 suggest, that she had set against him. Certainly the role of faction was important; her supporters at court were openly plotting against him, seeking to put pressure on Henry, to whom they had more access, and exploiting his weaknesses. He was finally dismissed over praemunire, a fourteenth-century law aimed at ensuring Papal law didn't supersede national laws; Wolsey couldn't defend himself. This was clearly an excuse to have him arrested. As Papal legate, responsible for the application of Papal laws in England, he must have been guilty under this statute for years.

The evidence from Sources 4 and 6 suggest that it was the issue of the divorce that led to Wolsey's downfall. Anne Boleyn had lost patience. However, there were also underlying factors. As Source 5 asserts, he was unpopular with practically everyone. However, it was the fact that the Boleyn faction increasingly had the confidence of the King that settled his fate. It may be that Henry began to trust them more, not only because of his feelings for Anne, but because they were always around him by 1529. Wolsey always worried when he was away from the King because he knew he had powerful enemies. Henry had started to go behind Wolsey's back after the Eltham Ordinances of 1526, which, in supposedly giving him Councillors always in attendance, ensured that these were always Wolsey's men. He had gone behind Wolsey's back, especially in matters of the divorce. For this reason it could be argued, as Hutchinson implies, that Wolsey's fall from power was only a matter of time and expected by some — and yet when it did come, it was a surprise. It needed Henry to lose confidence, as Wolsey knew he only maintained his position with Henry's support. It was therefore the failure to obtain an annulment that acted as a catalyst for his powerful enemies to convince Henry to dispense with Wolsey.

Integrates sources with own knowledge.

Reaches a conclusion based on discriminating use of evidence.

40/40
This is an excellent answer, which recognises the parameters of the question — it is about why Wolsey fell from power, not the divorce as such. This enables the candidate to examine the variety of factors that led to Wolsey's downfall and discuss how the failure to obtain the annulment was the excuse that his powerful enemies, who had the ear of Henry, could exploit. The sources are skilfully woven into the analysis.

Reverse engineering

The best essays are based on careful plans. Read the essay and the examiner's comments and try to work out the general points of the plan used to write the essay. Once you have done this, note down the specific examples used to support each general point.

Section 3: Henry's changing relations with the Catholic Church

The King's Great Matter

Henry VIII and Catherine of Aragon were a happy couple in their younger days, although tensions resulted from the unreliability of her Hapsburg relatives Ferdinand, Maximilian and later Charles V as allies. Catherine, at least publicly, had turned a blind eye to Henry's mistresses. However by 1525, Henry was thinking about an annulment of the marriage.

Reasons

- He was preoccupied by the need for an heir. It was clear Catherine was past childbearing age. She had gone through six pregnancies in fifteen years, but only one child had survived, their daughter Mary. Henry was very wary of a daughter inheriting the throne. The only previous example in England, that of Matilda in the Eleventh Century, had led to bloody Civil War.
- Catherine was growing old and had lost her looks.
- Henry, a deeply religious man, appears genuinely to have come to believe that his marriage was sinful. He had become aware of a Biblical extract in Leviticus that stated that one should not marry his dead brother's wife. Catherine had originally been married to his brother Arthur, who had died in 1502. Pope Julius II had given them special dispensation to marry. Henry came to believe that the Pope did not have the power to do this – and the infertility of the marriage was God's punishment.
- Henry had fallen in love with Anne Boleyn. Unlike other mistresses, she was encouraged by her powerful family, headed by the Duke of Norfolk, to hold out for marriage.

As Popes often gave dispensations and annulled marriages, Henry did not foresee any real problems. Indeed, in 1527 the Pope had annulled the marriage of Henry's sister, Margaret.

Complications

To this end, he sent Wolsey to obtain the necessary annulment. However, there were two complications:

- Pope Julius had given his special dispensation to override the theological objections to the marriage, and to rescind this would be to suggest he had been wrong to do so – thus countering the idea of Papal infallibility by which the Pope must always be right.
- Following the Hapsburg sack of Rome in 1527, the present Pope, Clement VII was effectively a prisoner of Charles V, Catherine's nephew. Charles knew that Catherine had been his most effective supporter at court and didn't want to lose her influence. Also, he was concerned with the loss of face to the Hapsburgs if the marriage was annulled.

As a result, Clement played for time. Two years passed with very little progress:

- Henry sought a **Papal bull** to allow him to marry a woman to whom he was already related, giving him permission to marry Anne Boleyn after having had an affair with her sister. He ended up with a worthless document saying he could marry a relative – so long as his existing marriage was declared invalid – which it wasn't.
- Henry tried to get Clement to establish a **Legatine Court** in England, to try the case of whether the marriage to Catherine was valid. He was determined the case should be settled in England, where he could control events, rather than in Rome.

Spot the mistake

Below are a sample exam-style part (a) question and a paragraph written in answer to the question. Why does this paragraph not get into Level 4? Once you have identified the mistake, rewrite the paragraph so that it displays the qualities of Level 4. The mark scheme on pages 4–5 will help you.

> How far do the sources suggest that Cardinal Campeggio had no intention of allowing the divorce to take place? Explain your answer using the evidence of Sources 1, 2 and 3.

> Cardinal Campeggio thinks it will be in vain to dissuade the King from the divorce and thinks the Queen will regard the whole affair with repugnance. He thinks then that he'll have his work cut out to get them to agree to the divorce but he'll try his hardest. If he had any intention of agreeing to the divorce, he would have been more positive. The King recognised he was delaying matters. In fact, Source 3 says it drove him to dementia.

SOURCE 1

(Letter from Cardinal Campeggio to Salviati, Bishop of Verona, secretary to Pope Clement VII, 29 February 1529)

I will do my utmost to persuade the King to abandon the divorce though I feel sure it will be in vain. I will do the same with the Queen who, I doubt not, will show her repugnance.

SOURCE 2

(From Polydore Vergil, History of England, written 1537)

But because the legate wasted time since they came to no decision, the suspicion then occurred to the King that they behaved thus on purpose to bring the business to nought in their court.

SOURCE 3

(JJ Scarisbrick, Henry VIII, published 1968)

Ever since he arrived, the legate had manufactured delays, refusing to take any decisive action until he had made every effort to reconcile the parties or before he had sent full reports to Rome. All this could take months. His loiterings, abetted by Clement, could drive his hosts to dementia.

Spectrum of significance

Below is a list of reasons why Henry wanted his marriage to Catherine to be annulled. Indicate their relative importance by writing their numbers on the spectrum below and justify your placement, explaining why some factors are more important than others.

1. Need for a male heir.
2. Fear of civil war if Mary became queen.
3. Catherine no longer attractive.
4. Religious belief that the marriage to Catherine was sinful.
5. Love for Anne Boleyn.
6. Desire to govern the English Church and abolish Papal authority.
7. Influence of the **Boleyn faction**.

Very important ←——————————————————→ Less important

Section 3: Henry's changing relations with the Catholic Church

Attempts to obtain an annulment

Henry's best chance for an annulment of the marriage came in the early part of 1528, when the Pope was relatively free and living in Oviedo and the French dominated Italy. The Pope sent Cardinal Campeggio to conduct the Legatine Court with Wolsey, but instructed him to delay any decision.

Meanwhile, the French lost the battle of Landriano in June 1529, and lost control of Italy. The Pope made the Treaty of Barcelona, allying himself with Charles V, and the outlook seemed bleak for a positive outcome to the Legatine Court. In July 1529, Campeggio declared that, as a Papal court, the Legatine Court must follow Roman holidays. He therefore declared it adjourned, with no decision made. This infuriated Henry's supporters and helped bring about the downfall of Wolsey.

Catherine of Aragon

Catherine had refused to acknowledge the authority of the court. Having been summoned to attend on the opening day, she made a great play of appealing to Henry directly and then walking out. She also made the annulment very difficult to achieve:

- Catherine may still have had feelings for Henry, but had too much pride and character to let herself be pushed aside.
- She was concerned that if her marriage was annulled, their daughter would be made illegitimate and removed from the succession. While Henry had qualms about queens ruling, she did not. Her own mother Isabella had been one of the strongest monarchs in Spanish history.
- Catherine maintained her marriage to Arthur had never been **consummated**, so Biblical rulings didn't apply. This was the crux of the matter, and clearly impossible to prove one way or the other. Henry maintained she had consummated her marriage to Arthur and she maintained she hadn't.
- Catherine was very popular in the country as a whole. Even when many of her supporters were kept away, two bishops were prepared to speak up for her when Parliament debated the issue of the divorce in 1531. The Ambassador from Milan said that there would be a rebellion if the King's marriage to Anne Boleyn went ahead.

Henry had previously sent agents to European universities to ask for their opinions on the issue. Given bribes, at least eight supported Henry. In July 1532, Henry judged that Papal dispensation was invalid because he argued that Catherine's marriage to Arthur had in fact been consummated.

Beginnings of Royal Supremacy

The Pope said the case should be heard in Rome, and Henry should attend. Henry had no intention of doing so. He felt the case should remain in England. The issue here was whose authority was greater – that of the monarch or that of the Pope?

In July 1533, the Pope decided that the marriage was valid and Henry must take Catherine back. However, by this time developments had made this ruling irrelevant. Having made his own judgement, Henry had annulled the marriage and secretly married Anne Boleyn in January 1533. This was necessary because she was pregnant.

Add own knowledge

Below are a sample exam-style part (b) question and the three sources referred to in the question. In one colour, draw links between the sources to show ways in which they agree about the importance of Catherine in preventing the divorce. In another colour, draw links between the sources to show ways they disagree. Around the edge of the sources, write relevant own knowledge. Again, draw links to show the ways in which this agrees and disagrees with the sources.

> Do you agree with the view that Catherine of Aragon was important in delaying the divorce from Henry VIII? Explain your answer using Sources 1, 2 and 3 and your own knowledge.

SOURCE 1

(Cardinal Campeggio, having received Catherine's confession, 28 October 1528. She gave him permission to publicise what she had said.)

She affirmed on her conscience that from 14 November when she was first espoused to the late prince Arthur to 2 April, following when he died, she did not sleep with him more than seven nights, and she remained intact as when she left the womb of her mother. It does not seem likely that she will bend her resolve either one way or the other.

SOURCE 2

(From JJ Scarisbrick, Henry VIII, *published 1968)*

Of course, Clement's subservience to Charles V, such as it was, presented an obstacle to Henry and may still have been one. But Clement's difficulty was not just that Charles was Catherine's nephew, but that Charles was Catherine's nephew and Henry's case a feeble one.

SOURCE 3

(From G Tremlett, Catherine of Aragon, *published 2010)*

Catherine's legal strategy was clear from the very start. The case had to be heard in Rome. She could not expect a fair trial from English judges, who would eventually bend to the King's will. This would be even more so if Wolsey, the King's right hand man, was the judge. In that case she would simply refuse to appear before the court.

Spot the inference

High-level answers avoid summarising or paraphrasing the sources, and instead make inferences from the sources. Below are a series of statements. Read Source 3 above and decide which of the statements:

- make inference from the source (I)
- paraphrase the source (P)
- summarise the Source (S)
- cannot be justified from the source (X).

Statement	I	P	S	X
Catherine believed she would have a fairer hearing in Rome because the judges would not be unduly influenced by the King.				
Catherine believed if the case was heard in Rome, she would win and the divorce would not be granted.				
If the case was heard in England, the judges would bend to the King's will.				
Catherine wanted the case to be heard in Rome. She could not expect a fair trial from English judges.				
Catherine hated Thomas Wolsey.				

Section 3: Henry's changing relations with the Catholic Church

From divorce to Royal Supremacy

Revised

Henry held an important conference at Hampton Court in August 1530, in which he discussed a collection of old documents entitled the **Sufficiently Abundant Collections,** which appeared to confirm that the monarchy had greater authority in England than the Pope. This gave Henry the authority he needed to declare his marriage invalid himself.

Royal Supremacy

Henry was determined on being absolute ruler of the Church. He agreed in 1531 to accept the title of The Supreme Head 'for as far as the word of God allows' – a phrase which clergy could interpret as they wished. However when Parliament in 1534 passed the Act of Supremacy there was no such qualification.

It was a short distance from the idea of Royal Supremacy to the break with Rome. In 1531, Henry accused the entire clergy of **praemunire**, fined them £100,000 and demanded they acknowledge him as Supreme Head of the Church in England. Many ask why this decision took so long to make.

Reasons

- After the fall of Wolsey, Henry was surrounded by nobles critical of clerical power – including the Boleyn faction and friends such as the Duke of Suffolk, who opposed the Church courts and also disliked senior Churchmen who tried to behave like aristocrats.
- Thomas Cromwell showed Henry how the law could be used to justify the decision. Cromwell drafted most of the legislation that confirmed the split with Rome.
- Anne Boleyn became pregnant and the marriage and legitimisation of the baby became urgent. In the event, Archbishop Cranmer declared the marriage to Catherine null and void on 23 May 1533, and on 28 May the marriage to Anne, which had secretly taken place in January, was announced. On 1 June, Anne Boleyn was crowned. With Catherine still popular there was little rejoicing outside the court.

The Royal Supremacy and subsequent **Reformation** took two forms:

- The creation of an English Church with coherent theology.
- The political revolution in which Henry made himself Head of the Church of England.

Political Reformation

The Reformation Parliament

The 'Reformation Parliament' met in 1529 and by 1535 had changed the English Church forever.

- It attacked Church abuses; acts were passed to limit **pluralcies** and non-residence of priests.
- It petitioned the King to stop bishops abusing their powers in the **Supplication against the Ordinaries**.
- It passed several crucial acts between 1532–34:
  – Conditional Restraint of Annates – taxes to Rome were ended and bishops had to be consecrated in England.
  – Act in Restraint of Appeals – all formal appeals were transferred to English courts instead of Rome. Henry was confirmed as Supreme Head of Church and State.
  – Ecclesiastical Appointments Act – bishops should be elected.
  – Dispensations Act – ('**Peter's Pence**') – the tax to Rome was abolished, and the Archbishop of Canterbury could grant all dispensations in England.
  – Act of Supremacy – Henry was given the power to define and punish heresy.
  – Succession and Treasons Act – Parliament sanctioned the divorce and allowed Henry to demand an oath acknowledging his supremacy – to refuse was high treason.

Identify an argument

Below are a series of definitions, a sample exam-style part (b) question and two sample conclusions. One of the conclusions achieves a high level because it contains an argument. The other achieves a lower level because it contains only description and assertion. Identify which is which. The mark scheme on pages 4–5 will help you.

- **Description:** a detailed account.
- **Assertion:** a statement of fact or an opinion, which is not supported by reason.
- **Reason:** a statement that explains or justifies something.
- **Argument:** an assertion justified with a reason.

Do you agree that the pregnancy of Anne Boleyn was the major factor in Henry's decision to break with Rome and declare himself Head of the English Church? Explain your answer using Sources 1 and 2 and your own knowledge.

Sample 1

As Source 2 shows, there is no doubt that Anne Boleyn's pregnancy created a greater sense of urgency in the question of the divorce and break with Rome. Henry was heartened also when he had met Francis I of France in 1532, and Anne was treated effectively as Queen. He desperately needed to legitimise their baby before it was born. However there are other factors. As Source 1 suggests, there were many financial and political advantages for Henry to take over the Church. Henry had already been persuaded that the king had greater authority over religious matters than the Pope. He had seen how easy it was for one man to control the Church in England, and he was more confident an autocrat than perhaps he had been in Wolsey's time in office. Henry must also have been influenced by the Reformation abroad, but even loyally Catholic monarchs such as Francis I and Charles V had wrested some control of their churches from the Pope. So while the pregnancy may have speeded matters, it was only one of several factors that led to the break with Rome.

Sample 2

Anne Boleyn fell pregnant with Henry's child. He had already decided to split with Rome. He had been convinced at the Hampton Conference that his authority was greater than that of the Pope. Cranmer, the Archbishop of Canterbury, told him he could just declare the marriage annulled because Henry was Head of the Church. This was much simpler than trying to persuade the Pope in Rome. The Pope was controlled for much of the time by Charles V, so he wouldn't give Henry his divorce. If Anne Boleyn had a male child, all Henry's problems would be over.

SOURCE 1

(From J Ross, The Tudors, *published 1979)*

For Henry himself the idea of becoming the Head of the Church of England was extremely attractive. The enormous wealth of the institutions would thereby be brought under his control, and the clergy would be obliged to conform to his jurisdiction. The king would become the one supreme authority, both spiritual and temporal, within the realm; the power of the Tudors would be universal.

SOURCE 2

(From D Wilson, A Brief History of Henry VIII, *published 2009)*

Any child of their union would have to be born, and preferably conceived in wedlock if its claim to the throne was to be uncontested. So when in mid-January 1533 Anne began to suspect that she was pregnant, something had to be done quickly. On or about 25 January, the couple were privately and very secretly married.

Section 3: Henry's changing relations with the Catholic Church

The role of key individuals

Revised

Three individuals played a key role in the development of the Reformation.

Anne Boleyn

Anne Boleyn was learned, with a real interest in theology, and may have influenced Henry in the Act of Supremacy if not in actual theology. Her ambitious family, headed by the Duke of Norfolk, sought to control the King through his love for Anne. However, she also introduced Henry to theological works such as those written by William Tyndale and Simon Fish which, while heretical, also argued that a King's authority in his own realm superseded that of the Pope. Anne encouraged churchmen with radical ideas such as Thomas Cranmer and Matthew Parker, and patronised those trying to disseminate Bibles in English even though they were banned. Because of Anne Boleyn, her family and circle, radical thinkers saw their influence extended throughout the court. It is no coincidence that all ten Bishops appointed while Anne was Queen were reformers.

Thomas Cranmer

Thomas Cranmer was a quiet, unassuming scholar who almost unwittingly developed much of the theoretical underpinning of the Reformation. He first came to Henry's attention in 1528, when he suggested applying to European universities for their rulings on the divorce. It was he who put much of the Sufficiently Abundant Collections together.

Henry was so pleased with Cranmer that he made him Archbishop of Canterbury in 1532. This made him the most important churchman in England. Cranmer embraced many of the new ideas. Indeed, he married the daughter of a leading German Protestant theologian, breaking his own vow of celibacy.

Cranmer worked closely with Thomas Cromwell, who shared his Protestant agenda in authorising an English Bible.

Thomas Cromwell

Like Wolsey, Cromwell was a commoner, so the nobles were always plotting against him. He drafted much of the legislation discussed in the previous topic; it was his job to drive it through Parliament and prevent any opposition from forming. In this sense, Cromwell was the real architect of the Reformation.

He was also the main instigator of the plot against the Boleyn faction. He gained most from their downfall, becoming Henry's **Lord Chancellor** and Vicar General (also known as vice-regent). The latter post gave him the same powers Wolsey had as legate, controlling the activities of the clergy. In 1536, in his general injunctions for example:

- He ordered them to defend the Royal Supremacy in their sermons.
- He ordered them to ensure children were taught the Lord's Prayer, Ten Commandments and Articles of Faith.

Cromwell was instrumental in the Dissolution of the Monasteries. In 1538, in his next set of injunctions he ordered the destruction of relics and religious images in churches, and authorised the English Bible to be read in churches. Cromwell did promote Protestant ideas in England. This was one of the accusations against him when he fell from power. After Cromwell, there was some restoration of Catholic theology to English churches with conservative churchmen controlling religious policy.

Develop the detail (a)

Below are a sample exam-style part (a) question and a paragraph written in answer to the question. The paragraph contains a limited amount of detail. Annotate the paragraph to add additional detail to the answer.

> How far do the sources agree about the significance of Thomas Cromwell in the political development of the English Reformation in the 1530s? Explain your answer using the evidence of Sources 1, 2 and 3.

Sources 1 and 3 agree that Thomas Cromwell's role was very significant. Source 1 says what an achievement the Reformation was and it was largely down to him. Source 3 shows that he drew up much of the legislation that changed the status of the Church. Source 2 on the other hand suggests he wasn't really responsible; the King was in control all the time and Cromwell might even be dismissed.

SOURCE 1

(From Bishop G Burnett, History of the Reformation of the Church of England, *published 1679)*

Cromwell's ministry was in constant course of flattery and submission; but by that he did great things that amaze one who has considered them well. The setting up the king's supremacy instead of usurpations of the Papacy and the rooting out of the monastic state in England, considering the wealth and zeal of the monks and friars in all the parts of the kingdom, as it was a very bold undertaking, so it was executed with great method and perfection in so short a time and with so few of the convulsions that might have been expected, that all this shows what a master he was, that could bring such a design to be finished in so few years with so little trouble or danger.

SOURCE 2

(From a letter from Du Marrilac, French Ambassador, on the arrest of Protestants, written on 10 April 1538)

Within a few days there will be seen in this country a great change in many things; which the King begins to make in his Ministers, recalling those he had rejected and degraded those he has raised.

Cromwell is tottering, for all those recalled, who were dismissed by his means, reserve not one good thought for him – among others the Bishops of Winchester, Durham and Bath, men of great learning and experience who are now summoned to the Privy Council.

SOURCE 3

(From JJ Scarisbrick, Henry VIII, *published 1968)*

That the 1530s were a decisive decade in English history was largely due to his [Cromwell's] energy and vision. He was immediately responsible for the vast legislative programme of the later sessions of the Reformation Parliament … he oversaw the break with Rome and the establishment of the Royal Supremacy.

Section 3: Henry's changing relations with the Catholic Church

Enforcing the Reformation

The political changes were largely peaceful, possibly because people were generally satisfied with Henry's rule. The biggest threat was the **Pilgrimage of Grace**, which will be covered in the next section. Because the opposition was relatively small, this made it easy to deal with.

Offenders were dealt with harshly, as a warning to others:

- 'The Holy Maid of Kent' Elizabeth Barton was renowned as a prophetess. In 1531 she threatened dire consequences if the King didn't return to Catherine. At this point Henry didn't feel strong enough to act against her. In 1533 however, having made the break from Rome, it was different. Elizabeth Barton was executed for treason.
- Various Franciscan Observants, an order of friars who it was felt owed particular allegiance to Rome, were burnt at the stake.
- Members of the Carthusian order of monks were also burnt.
- Bishop John Fisher and Sir Thomas More, the former Lord Chancellor, were executed in 1535 for refusing to accept the Oath of Supremacy.
- At the other religious extreme, William Tyndale, author of the New Testament in English, was burnt. So too was Robert Barnes, a reformist friar who had worked mainly in a diplomatic capacity for Henry for the best part of a decade.

The fact that the changes were political rather than religious may also explain the lack of opposition. Many Catholics such as Bishop Gardiner remained loyal, while reformers such as Cranmer often kept their theological beliefs secret. There was little support for the Pope in preference to Henry. A large crowd cheered when, in a mock battle on the Thames, the barge representing the Pope and his cardinals was sunk by that representing the King.

The Publication of the English Bible

The most significant change for most people was the publication of an English Bible. William Tyndale and Miles Coverdale had both produced English versions; the former, while superior, was regarded as too Protestant in outlook. In 1538, all churches were told to buy 'the Great Bible,' a blend of both the works. While the cost, at fourteen shillings, was huge, most churches complied. Many people welcomed the opportunity to read and discuss the Bible, while the illiterate were happy to have it read to them. In the past, religious leaders had argued lay people should not have access to Biblical texts because they wouldn't understand them.

Henry's role in the Reformation cannot be overemphasised. The Church itself played little active part in the proceedings. Henry might have been influenced by the likes of Anne Boleyn, Cranmer and Cromwell, but the settlement reached was largely of his own making. While Protestant ideas were spreading, the theology of the English Church remained largely Catholic, reflecting Henry's own preferences. When, for example, he said in 1539 that priests must remain celibate, Cranmer sent his wife back to Germany. Henry sought largely to continue Catholic theology.

Mind map

Use the information on the opposite page and your own knowledge to add detail to the mind map below, to show the extent of opposition to the divorce and royal supremacy.

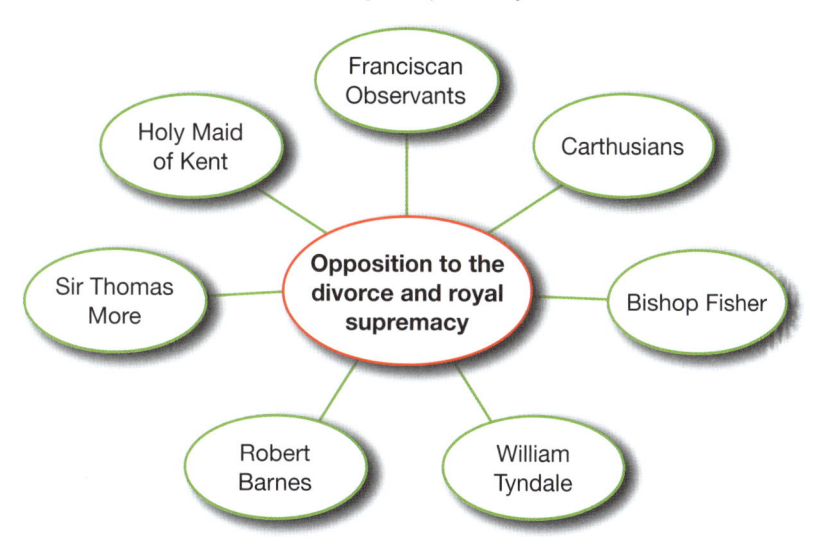

- Opposition to the divorce and royal supremacy
  - Franciscan Observants
  - Holy Maid of Kent
  - Carthusians
  - Sir Thomas More
  - Bishop Fisher
  - Robert Barnes
  - William Tyndale

Eliminate irrelevance

Below are a sample exam-style part (b) question and a paragraph written in answer to it. Read the paragraph and identify parts of the paragraph that are not directly relevant to the question. Draw a line through the information that is irrelevant and justify your deletions in the margin.

Do you agree with the view that Henry VIII was never fully committed to a Protestant Reformation? Explain your answer using Sources 1 and 2 and your own knowledge.

Henry VIII was prepared to go to great lengths to enforce his Protestant Reformation. This suggests that he was fully committed to the Protestant cause. For example, Source 1 refers to 'the martyrdom of priests', a reference to Henry's willingness to execute those who remained committed to the old ways. These priests included Bishop John Fisher who, with Sir Thomas More, was executed in 1535 for refusing to accept the Oath of Supremacy. One popular method of execution was burning at the stake. Some, such as Cranmer, avoided death by keeping their theology secret. Additionally, Source 2 refers to Henry throwing 'off the Pope's yoke', an anti-Catholic move which indicated that Henry was committed to Protestantism. This move was represented in a mock battle on the Thames in which the barge representing the Pope was sunk by the King's barge. Source 2 also says that 'the reformers offered him in their turn all the flatteries they could decently give' suggesting that they too were committed to bringing about religious change. In this sense, it is clear that there is evidence to support the view that Henry was genuinely committed to a Protestant Reformation in England.

SOURCE 1

(From E Ives, Will the Real Henry VIII Please Stand Up?, published 2006)

Henry met active opposition only in the north in 1536, and nobles who were deeply traditional in religion were active in suppressing it. As for the more populous parts, they would threaten revolt over taxes, but not over Henry's religious spoliation. Spectators might be shocked at the martyrdom of priests, but not sufficiently moved to try to save the martyrs.

SOURCE 2

(From Bishop G Burnett, History of the Reformation of the Church of England, published 1679)

When the King threw off the Pope's yoke, the reformers offered him in their turn all the flatteries they could decently give; and if they could have the patience to go no further than as he was willing to parcel out a reformation to them, he had perhaps gone further in it … He was all the time fluctuating; sometimes making steps for a reformation but then returning to his old notions.

Section 3: Henry's changing relations with the Catholic Church

The Ten Articles and the Six Articles

The Ten Articles

Henry acted as Head of the Church in consultation with theologians, but his patience became exhausted by their debates. He also feared Protestant ideas spreading from the continent, as they were heretical to him. Nevertheless the Ten Articles were passed in summer 1536 to ensure religious conformity. These were a brief statement of the Church's beliefs and moved away from some of the existing belief and practices in the Church in England. For example:

- They only mentioned three sacraments (baptism, penance and the Eucharist) whereas Catholics believed in seven sacraments.
- They contained some **Lutheran** ideas, such as Justification by Faith.
- The clergy were ordered to preach against the Pope.

The Bishop's Book

In order to give priests a much fuller explanation of what was to be believed and practised in July 1537, again in consultation with theologians and written mainly by Cranmer, The Bishop's Book was produced. This was more conservative, and restored the other four sacraments (matrimony, confirmation, holy orders and extreme unction). However, it placed emphasis on scriptural rather than Papal authority – the idea that authority came from the text of the Bible, rather than what the Pope decided. Its main purpose was to inform the clergy what the teaching of the **Henrican Church** actually was.

The Acts of Six Articles, 1539

The Six Articles marked a return to Catholic theology in an English Church.

- They asserted the doctrine of transubstantiation, clerical celibacy and private masses.
- There were harsh punishments for offenders, and within a few weeks 500 had been arrested for heresy.

Destruction of religious relics and images

While Henry appeared genuinely to want a national Church based on Catholic principles, he was anxious to stamp out the types of abuses that had led to the Reformation on the continent. From 1538, in a new set of Injunctions, Cromwell sent out Commissioners to destroy relics and images. Often, the Church had charged significant amounts of money for displaying relics that were said to perform miracles. Many had been in awe of the Holy Rood of Bexley, a figure of Christ fitted with strings by which the priest could move the eyes and lips. This was taken to London and enthusiastically destroyed. More seriously, the shrine of **Thomas Becket** was wrecked. Becket was no longer venerated as a saint, but condemned as a traitor. Veneration of saints was discouraged. This heartened those reformers such as Hugh Latimer, Bishop of Worcester who wished to encourage more Protestant ideas.

As an example of the ascendancy of more Protestant thinkers, the conservative Bishop Gardiner was removed from Council in June 1539. Henry allowed himself to be persuaded by Cromwell that a Protestant alliance was advantageous, to be cemented by a marriage to Anne of Cleves. However the subsequent infighting at court and Henry's disappointment with his bride led to the fall of Cromwell and return of the conservative churchmen such as Gardiner who wished to restore Catholic theology.

You're the examiner

Below are a sample exam-style part (a) question and a paragraph written in answer to this question. Read the paragraph and the mark scheme provided on pages 4–5. Decide which level you would award the paragraph. Write the level below, along with a justification for your choice.

> How far do Sources 1, 2 and 3 suggest that the Church was corrupt and in need of reform? Explain your answer using the evidence of Sources 1, 2 and 3.

Source 1 tells us that covetousness is the root of all evil, and there was a lot of covetousness in the Church. Priests had multiple benefices, while they quarrelled about tithes, a tax-like payment to the Church. The Hunne case shows how unfair the mortuary, a tax on the burial of the dead could be – the priest demanded as payment the burial robe of Richard Hunne's baby. Source 3 agrees. It mentions the Holy Rood, which was supposed to be a miraculous crucifix on which Christ could speak – but it was only a priest pretending. Robert Aske disagrees. He talks about the good things about the Church, how the abbeys help travellers in inhospitable places and offer spiritual guidance.

Level: Reasons for choosing this level:
_____
_____

Recommended reading

Below is a list of suggested further reading on the topic of the Reformation:

- David H Pill, *The English Reformation 1529–58*, parts 2–3 (1973).
- Robert Hutchinson, *Thomas Cromwell*, chapters 3–4 (2007).
- J R H Moorman, *A History of the Church in England*, pp161–76 (1973).
- Glyn Redworth, 'Whatever Happened to the English Reformation?', History Today, Vol. 37, (Oct 1987).
- www.thereformation.info/english_reformation Index.htm. This is a useful and comprehensive website, with many original documents transcribed.

SOURCE 1

(Sermon by John Colet, 1512)

O Covetousness: Paul rightly called thee 'the root of all evil'. For from thee comes all this piling up of benefices one on top of the other; from thee come the great pensions, assigned out of many benefices resigned, from thee quarrels about tithes, about offerings, about mortuaries.

SOURCE 2

(From Robert Aske, leader of the Pilgrimage of Grace, written 1537)

The northern abbeys gave great alms to the poor and served God well. Many were in the mountains and desert places, where the people were poor and ignorant. The abbeys gave them food for their bodies and spiritual guidance by the example set in the lives of the monks and by education and preaching.

SOURCE 3

(From H Ellis, Original Letters Illustrative of English History, *1824–46)*

I found in the image of the rood called the Rood of Grace, which heretofore hath been had in great veneration, certain engines and old wire, with old rotten sticks in the back of same that did cause the eyes of the same to move and stare in the head thereof like unto a lively thing and also the nether lip in likewise to move as though it could speak.

Section 3: Henry's changing relations with the Catholic Church

Section 3: Exam focus

Revised

On pages 53–55 are sample A-grade answers to the exam-style questions on these two pages. Read the answers and the examiner's comments around them.

a) How far do Sources 1, 2 and 3 suggest that supporters of Catherine of Aragon delayed the annulment of her marriage to Henry? Explain your answer using the evidence of Sources 1, 2 and 3.

b) Do you agree with the view that the most important changes in the 1530s were in the creation of the Royal Supremacy rather than in religious belief? Explain your answer, using Sources 4, 5 and 6 and your own knowledge.

SOURCE 1

(Letter from the Spanish Ambassador de Mendoza to Charles V, 4 February 1529)

Have just heard that the King has pressed the legates so urgently to have the cause decided here that they have sent two secretaries to the Pope and have given the King great hope of a favourable answer. The King is so hot upon it that there is nothing he does not promise to gain his end and if the cause be tried here it may be considered as lost, for I have as little trust in the new legate as the old one. Campeggio has done nothing for the Queen as yet, except to press her to enter religion.

SOURCE 2

(Letter from Charles V to the Bishop of Burgos, 6 February 1529)

Hears by various ways of the utmost efforts made by the King of England to divorce from his Queen, the Emperor's aunt, a thing which grieves him deeply, especially in the present scandalous state of the Christian Commonwealth. Believes it must arise from the sinister persuasions of some who are about him. Had no doubts it will grieve all good subjects of the kingdom who know the marriage was made with express permission of the Holy See and had remained unquestioned so many years. The Emperor is compelled for his part to support his aunt and had given charge to his Ambassador accordingly. He had also prayed to the Pope that the case may be determined in his consistory and not in England.

SOURCE 3

(From G Tremlett, Catherine of Aragon, *published 2010)*

Even then she could not bring herself to criticise the King, at least not in writing. That would have been too dangerous. He was a good and virtuous man at heart, she insisted in one of the deluge of letters she began sending to her nephew Charles. The Pope, by delaying judgement had allowed her enemies in the Boleyn camp to take him prisoner … Catherine's own supporters meanwhile were terrified. 'They have scared them so much that they dare not speak,' she complained. She had already noticed that the waverers were being drawn over by royal offerings 'like hawks to the lure'. Catherine felt humiliated.

SOURCE 4

(From K Randell, Henry VIII and the Reformation of England, *published 2001)*

So was the Royal Supremacy of any great significance? It seems that it was because, with hindsight, historians have been able to detect that it marked a dramatic shift in the balance of power within the state. By the 1530s the secular arm was definitely the dominant partner … However it was clear that the Church was still a major force within the land but it rapidly declined in both political and constitutional importance after 1534. Church courts continued in existence but they no longer offered any challenge to their civil counterparts and Church men largely ceased to play a prominent part in political affairs.

SOURCE 5

(From G Redworth, Whatever Happened to the English Reformation?, *published 1987))*

Henry was capable of making up his own mind concerning the direction of religious policy, that is whenever he felt the urge to be decisive. During the drafting of the Act of the Six Articles of 1539, which reaffirmed the English position of maintaining essential Catholic doctrine despite the break with Rome, the King overturned the opinion of the majority of his prelates by deciding that confession was not necessary according to the law of God.

SOURCE 6

(From the Act of the Six Articles, 1539)

First, that in the most blessed sacrament of the altar is present really under the form of bread and wine, the natural blood and body of our saviour, Jesus Christ.

Thirdly, that priests … may not marry by the law of God.

Marriages of priests and professed persons are declared void.

Persons who refuse to confess or to receive the sacrament shall be fined and imprisoned by the King's Council.

a) How far do Sources 1, 2 and 3 suggest that supporters of Catherine of Aragon delayed the annulment of her marriage to Henry?

Explain your answer using the evidence of Sources 1, 2 and 3.

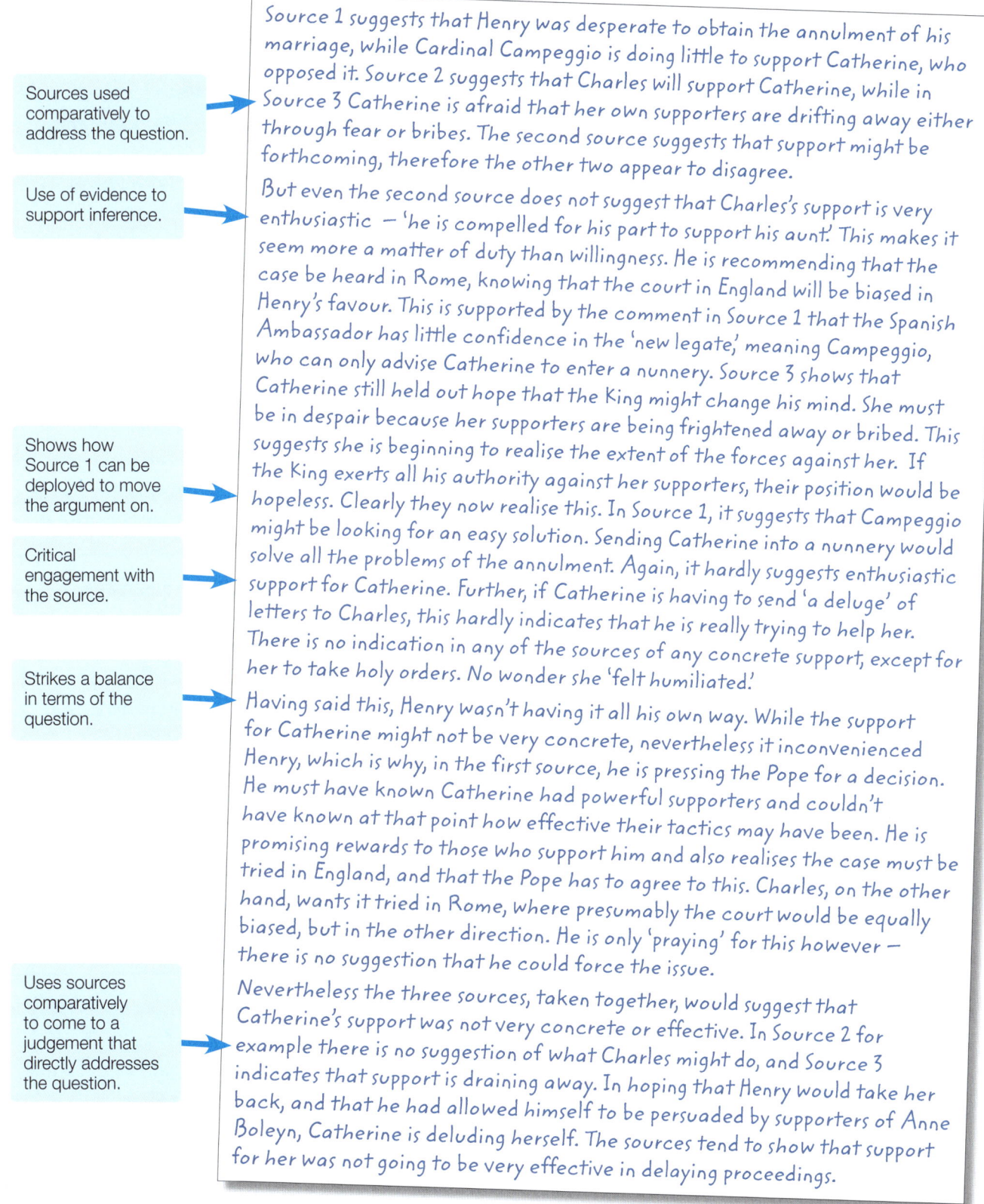

> Source 1 suggests that Henry was desperate to obtain the annulment of his marriage, while Cardinal Campeggio is doing little to support Catherine, who opposed it. Source 2 suggests that Charles will support Catherine, while in Source 3 Catherine is afraid that her own supporters are drifting away either through fear or bribes. The second source suggests that support might be forthcoming, therefore the other two appear to disagree.
>
> But even the second source does not suggest that Charles's support is very enthusiastic — 'he is compelled for his part to support his aunt'. This makes it seem more a matter of duty than willingness. He is recommending that the case be heard in Rome, knowing that the court in England will be biased in Henry's favour. This is supported by the comment in Source 1 that the Spanish Ambassador has little confidence in the 'new legate', meaning Campeggio, who can only advise Catherine to enter a nunnery. Source 3 shows that Catherine still held out hope that the King might change his mind. She must be in despair because her supporters are being frightened away or bribed. This suggests she is beginning to realise the extent of the forces against her. If the King exerts all his authority against her supporters, their position would be hopeless. Clearly they now realise this. In Source 1, it suggests that Campeggio might be looking for an easy solution. Sending Catherine into a nunnery would solve all the problems of the annulment. Again, it hardly suggests enthusiastic support for Catherine. Further, if Catherine is having to send 'a deluge' of letters to Charles, this hardly indicates that he is really trying to help her. There is no indication in any of the sources of any concrete support, except for her to take holy orders. No wonder she 'felt humiliated.'
>
> Having said this, Henry wasn't having it all his own way. While the support for Catherine might not be very concrete, nevertheless it inconvenienced Henry, which is why, in the first source, he is pressing the Pope for a decision. He must have known Catherine had powerful supporters and couldn't have known at that point how effective their tactics may have been. He is promising rewards to those who support him and also realises the case must be tried in England, and that the Pope has to agree to this. Charles, on the other hand, wants it tried in Rome, where presumably the court would be equally biased, but in the other direction. He is only 'praying' for this however — there is no suggestion that he could force the issue.
>
> Nevertheless the three sources, taken together, would suggest that Catherine's support was not very concrete or effective. In Source 2 for example there is no suggestion of what Charles might do, and Source 3 indicates that support is draining away. In hoping that Henry would take her back, and that he had allowed himself to be persuaded by supporters of Anne Boleyn, Catherine is deluding herself. The sources tend to show that support for her was not going to be very effective in delaying proceedings.

Sources used comparatively to address the question.

Use of evidence to support inference.

Shows how Source 1 can be deployed to move the argument on.

Critical engagement with the source.

Strikes a balance in terms of the question.

Uses sources comparatively to come to a judgement that directly addresses the question.

20/20

This answer skilfully blends the sources to arrive at a valid judgement. The sources are cross-referenced and compared critically. Elements where they challenge each other are analysed. The candidate engages with them critically to make valid comments about Catherine's predicament and goes beyond the superficial to arrive at deeper meanings.

Section 3: Henry's changing relations with the Catholic Church

b) Do you agree with the view that the most important changes in the 1530s were in the creation of the Royal Supremacy rather than in religious belief? Explain your answer, using Sources 4, 5 and 6 and your own knowledge.

Introduction addresses question.

After some years of confusion and dispute, the Act of the Six Articles clearly emphasised that Catholic practices should continue in the English Church. However, Henry had made himself Head of the Church by the Act of Supremacy, so he was both Head of the Church and of the Government. On the surface this marked a great change, because one of the arguments against the presence of the Church was that it had held too much power independently of the state. Wolsey had fallen on the charge of praemunire, that is, following Papal laws that superseded those of the state. In fact in 1531, Henry had accused the entire clergy of this and fined them accordingly.

Comparative analysis of sources.

Source 4 suggests that, while the Church was still influential, the Royal Supremacy had marked a dramatic shift to increasing the power of the state, while Source 5 shows the influence of Henry in drafting the Six Articles. It gives the example of Confession, which was maintained as the sixth article, which Henry believed no longer had to be made to a priest. In this sense, Henry would have reduced the role of the priesthood. Source 4 moreover shows that the power of Church courts was reduced; their influence was one of the main causes of anti-clericalism in England, as the example of Richard Hunne had shown as early as 1511.

Balance attempted with Henry's religious ideas.

The Act of Supremacy and the Six Articles, as exemplified in the extracts in Source 6, showed that while Henry wanted to take control of the Church, he wasn't looking to change its theology. They appear to mark a success for those of his advisers who supported traditional beliefs such as Bishop Gardiner. Indeed, within a short time, five hundred people had been arrested for heretical beliefs. However, Scarisbrick showed that the Articles really indicated that Henry was making a point for Church unity, and Lutheran and Protestant ideas continued — indeed as in the case of confession, Henry may even have been coming to support them. Having said this, as can be seen in Source 6, he was absolutely adamant on the crucial doctrine of transubstantiation or the real presence in the Eucharist, and people who disputed this risked execution. Other Catholic ideas such as clerical celibacy and purgatory were continued. The Archbishop of Canterbury, Cranmer, sent his wife back to Germany.

Introduces own knowledge.

Source 4 argues that the state gained in importance at the expense of the Church, which Henry had been determined to take control of. The example of the decline of Church courts is given. Henry sought power for himself. Historians no longer believe that Cromwell wished Henry to share power with Parliament. When the Act of Supremacy was passed in 1534, it was confirmed by Parliament and gave Henry absolute power over the Church. Cromwell was appointed as Vicar General, in charge of the clergy, whom he actively supervised — as in promoting the use of an English Bible and getting the Bishops to agree doctrine. However, as Source 5 argues, it was Henry who largely determined that doctrine, although he did sanction debate. Moreover, while the sources may seem concerned with control of the Church and religious issues, Henry controlled the political reformation. Parliament had passed a series of acts in the 1530s to facilitate the break with Rome. These included the Conditional Restraint of Annates, by which taxes to Rome were ended, except for a 5 per cent token payment. Bishops had to be consecrated in England. The Act in Restraint of Appeals meant all formal appeals were transferred to English courts and appeals to Rome were disallowed. Henry was confirmed as Supreme Head of Church and State. The Ecclesiastical Appointments Act set out how Bishops should be elected. There was also the Dispensations Act, by which 'Peter's Pence,' the tax to Rome, was abolished. The Archbishop of Canterbury was given the authority to grant all dispensations in England. In addition, with the Succession Act, Parliament sanctioned the divorce and made it possible for Henry to demand an oath acknowledging his supremacy — to refuse was high treason.

Detailed knowledge in support of the argument.

Clearly, this raft of legislation gave Henry complete authority over the Church. In addition, in having the authority to define heresy, he had the power, should he wish, to dictate doctrine. However, some historians have argued that the power of the Church was diminishing in nation states already. The Pope had not intervened often in English internal affairs, and very few people had the necessary funds to appeal to Rome over national courts. In this sense, it could be argued that it was the issue of the divorce that had led to the break. The Church had not exacted massive amounts of money to be sent to Rome — 'Peter's Pence' amounted to only a few hundred pounds a year.

Henry did not seek to impose his will on theological matters necessarily, so long as the basic Catholic tenets were continued, as is shown by terms of the Six Acts and reinforced in the analysis in Source 5. However, he was an absolute monarch and this was reflected in the Government and influence of the Church. Source 4 shows that members of the clergy no longer became senior government ministers in Henry's reign. While, for example, Wolsey had been both a senior churchman and government minister, Cromwell was a layman and Cranmer, as Archbishop of Canterbury, had little role in the running of the Government. With the possible exception of Gardiner, Henry kept churchmen and politicians in separate spheres as far as possible — except for Cromwell as Vicar General, who reflected Henry's will and acted as Henry's agent. One could argue therefore that the Royal Supremacy was more significant than theological change in the 1530s. If the English Reformation was in two parts, first the state control of the Church and secondly changes in religious beliefs, Henry was far more concerned with the first issue than the latter.

Uses sources and own knowledge to come to a valid and reasoned judgement in terms of the question.

40/40

This is well argued, using sources critically and even commenting on their limitations in terms of the debate. Their use is effectively augmented by own knowledge to come to a valid, supported conclusion in terms of the question. Focus is maintained and the evidence is analysed effectively throughout.

Reverse engineering

The best essays are based on careful plans. Read the essay and the examiner's comments and try to work out the general points of the plan used to write the essay. Once you have done this, note down the specific examples used to support each general point.

Section 4:
The Dissolution of the Monasteries

The Visitations and the Valor Ecclesiasticus of 1535

The Dissolution of the Monasteries

It is generally agreed that there were three crucial reasons for the Dissolution of the Monasteries:

- Henry needed money to fund his foreign policies and wars.
- The monasteries were potentially a source of opposition to his **Reformation** because most owed allegiance to parent institutions abroad.
- Henry saw he could buy allegiance to his religious and political changes by selling off church lands, thus binding the purchasers to them. If England became Catholic again, the lands they paid for could be restored to the original owners.

There were about 850 monastic houses in England and Wales in 1530. Some were friaries, where the inmates went out and did good works in the community. Others were closed, where inmates were supposed to live a life of quiet contemplation. All came under the authority of Thomas Cromwell as Vicar General.

There were two separate major surveys of the monasteries in 1535, the Visitations and Valor Ecclesiasticus. Thomas Cromwell was responsible for the organisation of both.

The Visitations

Two of Cromwell's most trusted officials, Richard Layton and Thomas Legh, were sent to inspect the monasteries in terms of the conduct and behaviour of the monks and nuns. They were tireless in their efforts, but may have emphasised that evidence which supported what Cromwell had told them to find. While they did not exactly falsify evidence, they were biased and also interpreted data unfairly.

They found considerable evidence of immorality, corruption and irreligious behaviour. Their methods were regarded as unfair – they asked loaded questions and amassed huge amounts of data on the basis of short visits.

The Valor Ecclesiasticus

This was possibly initiated by Henry himself, and was a far more ambitious exercise. It was an attempt to record all the wealth owned by the monasteries. It was completed by unpaid commissioners, normally local gentry in a six-month period, and gave a detailed picture both of monastic wealth and the income of individual clerics

The Valor Ecclesiasticus found that most religious houses were endowed with estates. Often, over the centuries, people had willed lands to the monasteries in return for remission from **purgatory**. While reformer Simon Fish had exaggerated when he said the clergy owned 33 per cent of England's landed property, later writers do estimate the monasteries were in possession of 5–17 per cent. Their total income was over £160,000 a year and brought in three times more than the royal estates. Westminster Abbey was the richest with an income of £3,912; many of the smallest had less than £20 per year.

As landlords, the monasteries had many other rights, such as the ability to collect tolls for markets held on their estates, while they exploited the natural resources by selling timber and diverting the course of rivers.

The Valor Ecclesasticus was clearly good news for Henry. He was Supreme Head of the Church – therefore technically in control of the monasteries – and a monarch desperately in need of money.

Spot the inference (a)

High-level answers avoid summarising or paraphrasing the sources, and instead make inferences from the sources. Below is a series of statements. Read Source 2 below and decide which of the statements:

- make the inference from the source (I)
- paraphrase the source (P)
- summarise the source (S)
- cannot be justified from the source (X).

Statement	I	P	S	X
Smaller monasteries were being particularly singled out as being sinful places.				
Smaller monasteries were being picked on because they were easier to close.				
Smaller monasteries were sinful places where the property was wasted.				
All monks and nuns in smaller religious houses lived dissolute lives.				
Open sin and disgusting living were daily occurrences in smaller monasteries.				

Write the question (a)

The following sources relate to the amount of abuse and corruption in the monasteries. Read the information on the page opposite. Having done this, write an exam-style part (a) question using the sources.

SOURCE 1

(From Robert Layton, Ecclesiastical Commissioner, writing about the Abbot at Langden in Kent)

[The Abbot] passes all that ever I knew in profound bawdy: the drunkenest knave living. All his canons are as he is, not one spark of virtue amongst them; arrant bawdy knaves every one. The abbot caused his chaplain to take a whore; brought her into his own chamber; took one of the featherbeds off his own bed in the inner chamber and there caused him to go to bed with her.

SOURCE 2

(From the First Act for the Dissolution of the Monasteries, 1536)

Open sin and disgusting living is daily used and committed amongst the little and small abbeys and priories and other religious houses of monks and nuns where their number is under twelve. These religious houses spoil, destroy and waste their property.

SOURCE 3

(From K Randell, Henry VIII and the Reformation in England, *published 2001)*

The 'bottom up' historians have also shown that the state of the monasteries in the 1530s was not nearly so bad as Protestant writers have generally maintained. Their conclusion has been that, although less than 10 per cent of houses were centres of spiritual fervour, the vast majority were following the way of life prescribed by the order to which they belonged. In particular they have established that the **comperta** resulting from the Visitations of 1535 must be treated with extreme caution.

Section 4: The Dissolution of the Monasteries

The dissolution of the smaller monasteries, 1536

It is not known which was the prime mover, but with the evidence of the two surveys, Henry and Cromwell undoubtedly agreed that this was too good an opportunity to pass. Cromwell drew up legislation to close the smaller monastic houses. The Dissolution of the Monasteries Act was passed in 1536. Cromwell wanted to move quickly, before the houses had time to move their assets.

- The Dissolution Bill used the evidence of immorality as its justification. This issue dominated the preamble, written by Cromwell. Henry chose to believe the stories of immorality, because they gave him the excuse and deflected opinion away from the motive of greed.
- The act closed down all monastic houses with an income of less than £200 per year. All their incomes and benefices passed to the Crown. In all, 376 houses were closed.
- The inmates were scattered. Monks could transfer to other monasteries or take a pension. Many found employment as parish priests. Nuns were not so lucky, and usually applied to join other convents.
- Dissolution was not unprecedented. Wolsey suppressed 29 monasteries to finance Cardinal's College and the school at Ipswich; while wholesale closures took place in European lands under Protestant control.
- There were 67 known exemptions. Officially, the reason given was because of the good works such houses undertook. In reality it was either because the authorities were heavily bribed, or because the abbots had influential friends.

Impact

- There was concern that the poor would suffer because of the loss of the charitable functions of the monasteries. However, the act said that the new owners should maintain hospitality and also continue to farm the land as before, so unemployment would be minimised.
- It was found that monasteries had spent less than 3 per cent of their income on charitable works, so their role in terms of helping the poor was probably exaggerated. Certainly, few monasteries spent the 33 per cent that was recommended by many Orders.
- The wealth from the monasteries went to the Crown. Cromwell is alleged to have told Henry he would make him the richest king in Christendom, but it is unlikely Henry needed to be told.
- Others had different ideas. Anne Boleyn, for example, had presumed some of the wealth would be used to endow educational institutions. Her chaplain, John Skip, preached a sermon at court on the dangers of greed and warned the King about taking poor advice, presumably referring to Cromwell. There was, however, no doubt in Henry's mind that the revenue belonged to the King.

It is widely believed that there was little reaction to the dissolutions, because the monasteries were already in decline. People were rushing to buy their lands before even the legislation was complete. Undoubtedly, the ease with which the smaller houses were closed gave encouragement to the King in his later decision to close them all.

Linking sources

Below are a sample exam-style part (a) question and the three sources referred to in the question. In one colour, draw links between the sources to show ways in which they agree about the Dissolution of the Monasteries. In another colour, draw links between the sources to the ways in which they disagree.

> How far do Sources 1, 2 and 3 agree that the Dissolution of the Monasteries was effectively a ploy by which the Government gained control of Church lands? Explain your answer, using the evidence of Sources 1, 2 and 3.

Eliminate irrelevance

a

Below is a paragraph written in answer to the question in 'linking sources' above. Read the paragraph and identify those parts of it that are not directly related to the question. Draw a line through the information that is irrelevant and justify your deletions in the margin.

> Sources 1, 2 and 3 all agree that the Dissolution of the Monasteries was essentially a land grab. Cromwell had promised to make Henry as rich as Croesus. Croesus was a fabulously rich king in Greek mythology, who was defeated by the Persians in the Fifth Century BC. Source 1 is an example of the instructions given to the Commissioners to enquire as to the wealth of monasteries, while Source 2 is an example of what they found. It's a pity they're not about the same place, but they do show how rich Henry could become if he was going to acquire all the wealth from the monasteries. Source 3 suggests he would be £100,000 a year better off. That may not seem that much to us when he has a country to run, but prices were much lower in those days so it would be millions and millions in today's values. In this way, the sources clearly indicate that the Dissolution of the Monasteries was a land grab because they all stress the wealth that the dissolution will bring to the King.

SOURCE 1

(Instructions to commissioners appointed in 1536 to survey the smaller monasteries in the bishopric of Llandaff)

Item, to examine the true yearly value of all the farms of the same house, deducting thereof rents resolute [paid], pensions and portions paid out of the same ... bailiffs, receivers, stewards and auditors' fees and the name of them to whom they be due and none other.

Item, what leases have been made to any farmer, of the farms pertaining to the same house, and what rent is reserved, and to whom and for how many years, and a copy of the indenture if they can get it or else the counterpane.

SOURCE 2

(Extract from the Valor Ecclesiasticus, Priory of Maxstoke)

Income received from churches appropriated to the priory	**Total** £27: 17s: 0d
Fixed rents	**Total** 8s: 6 1/2 d
Income from lands, tenements, meadows, grazing and pasture	**Total** £42: 16s: 2d

SOURCE 3

(From D Wilson, A Brief History of Henry VIII, published 2009)

Cromwell turned Henry VIII into a modern Croesus. Crown revenues increased by over £100,000 p.a. [per year], which was more than the total income the Government had received in 1530.

Section 4: The Dissolution of the Monasteries

The Pilgrimage of Grace

While the Dissolution of the Monasteries hadn't attracted significant opposition elsewhere, it was an important factor in the **Pilgrimage of Grace**, which was the only major rebellion in Henry's reign. The Pilgrimage of Grace was the central event in a series of rebellions that took place in 1536, firstly in Lincolnshire and then across Yorkshire and the north-west.

Reasons

The reasons were varied and complex, often dependent on local factors. There was little coordination between the rebellions. However, religion and the Dissolution of the Monasteries was one common factor.

- There were the underlying factors of social and economic unrest. Harvests had been poor in recent years.
- Local nobles felt marginalised. Henry's Government seemed distant.
- There were lots of rumours that the Government was going to confiscate all the wealth of the Church, including valuables in the parish churches. The presence of three sets of commissioners in Lincolnshire sparked off the original uprising.
- There was resentment against low-born bureaucrats such as Cromwell, who it was felt were misleading the King.
- There were concerns about the religious reforms; many of the rebels were loyal Catholics who believed the spread of new ideas to be heresy.

The Pontefract articles

Robert Aske, a Yorkshire lawyer, was instrumental in drawing up the **Pontefract Articles** in December 1536 – the closest the rebels got to a manifesto. It focused largely on wishing to return to the situation before the Reformation:

- The divorce from Catherine was condemned: Mary should be legitimised.
- The King's evil counsellors should be dismissed.
- There should be a parliament in the north.
- The Dissolution of the Monasteries should be reversed.
- The breach with Rome should be reversed.

End of the rebellion

The rebellion would have been more serious had the Pope intervened. He had instructed Cardinal Pole, a member of the leading Yorkist family, to organise an invasion. However, before Pole could act, the rebellion was over. Henry took advantage and executed other senior members of the Pole family, including the elderly matriarch, the Countess of Salisbury.

Henry was saved by the very loyalty of the rebels. Their real intention was to save him from evil advisors, and they believed he would listen to their petitions. Aske himself held back more radical colleagues. Henry had no compunction in lying and giving false hopes to put the rebellion down. Therefore his policies were to play for time by promising anything, hoping the rebels would disperse when they thought they'd achieved their objectives – and then exact revenge. An army under Norfolk was sent north. When the rebels went home, they arrested them at their leisure.

However, it must be remembered that Henry had no permanent army or police force. Any rebellion was a threat. He was always mindful of the turbulence of the Wars of the Roses, and the efforts of Henry VII to secure the dynasty. In his own mind, for the safety and security of the realm he had to be completely ruthless.

Mind map

Use the information on the opposite page and your own knowledge to add detail to the mind map below about the reasons for the Pilgrimage of Grace and why it failed.

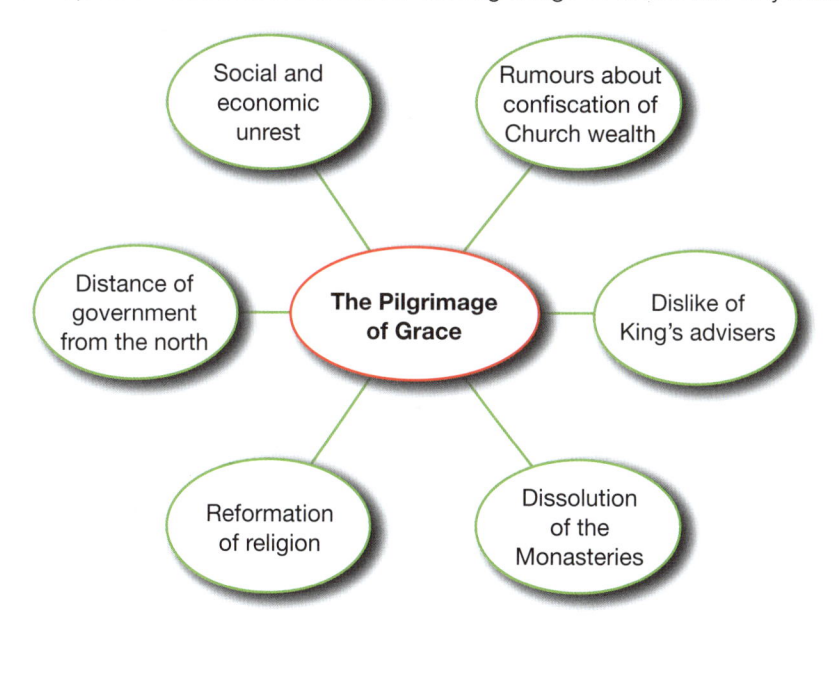

- Social and economic unrest
- Rumours about confiscation of Church wealth
- Distance of government from the north
- **The Pilgrimage of Grace**
- Dislike of King's advisers
- Reformation of religion
- Dissolution of the Monasteries

Explain the difference

Sources 1 and 2 give different interpretations of the Pilgrimage of Grace. List the ways in which the sources differ. Explain the differences between the sources, using the provenance of the sources alone. The provenance appears at the top of the source in brackets.

SOURCE 1

(From Robert Aske, The Oath of Honourable Men, drawn up in 1536)

Ye shall not enter into this, our Pilgrimage of Grace for the Commonwealth, but only for the love you do bear unto Almighty God his faith, and to the holy Church militant and the maintenance thereof, to the preservation of the King's person and his issue, to the purifying of the nobility and to expulse all villain blood and evil counsellors against the Commonwealth from his grace and Privy Council the same.

SOURCE 2

(Instructions from Henry VIII to the Earl of Derby, charged with putting down the rebellion in the north-west)

[Put down] an insurrection attempted about the Abbey of Sawley in Lancashire, where the abbot and monks have been restored by traitors. We now desire you immediately to repress it, to apprehend the captains and either have them immediately executed as traitors or sent up to us. We leave it however, to your discretion to go elsewhere in case of greater emergency. You are to take the said abbot and monks forthwith with violence and have them hanged without delay in their monks' apparel.

Section 4: The Dissolution of the Monasteries

The dissolution of the larger monasteries

At some point during 1537, Henry and Cromwell decided on a complete dissolution. They began with those in the North, which had offered any support for the Pilgrimage of Grace. The head of each house was declared a traitor, and their assets were forfeit to the Crown. Monks and nuns were forced to leave. However this still left all those houses who hadn't rebelled. These were closed in 1538 and 1540, with Waltham Abbey being the last to close in March 1540.

The process
- Henry sent out commissioners to different parts of the country, to inform the monasteries that they were voluntarily expected to close and surrender their assets to the Crown.
- At the same time all the friaries were closed until by March 1539, there were no friars left in England.
- There was comparatively little resistance and harsh penalties for those who did protest. The Abbots of Glastonbury, Colchester and Reading were executed after having had very dubious accusations made against them, such as denying the king's supremacy.
- The Abbot of Colchester had claimed that, following the terms of the 1536 Act suppressing the smaller monasteries, it was illegal to suppress houses of more than £200 per year. Therefore in 1539, Parliament passed a second Dissolution Act to address this.

Sales
There is some evidence that Cromwell had preferred to lease monastery lands and guarantee an income for the Crown independent of Parliamentary sanction. However, Henry wanted cash. In December 1539, the **Court of Augmentations** began to sell land. However, it wasn't until 1543–47 that two-thirds of the sales took place, because of the huge expense of fighting wars against France.

Effects of the Dissolution of the Monasteries
- Clearly the culture that monasteries had brought to England was lost. However, there is evidence that monastic life was already in decline.
- A few monks were absorbed into the parish system, for example becoming parish priests. Few went to parent houses abroad. Nuns had a more difficult time and little is known about what happened to them. Because of their vow of chastity, which was still binding, they weren't allowed to marry. Some may have gone back to their families. Monastic servants were usually employed by the new owners of the former religious houses.
- Little of the revenue was spent on education or the Church. There was wholesale vandalism of the monastic buildings, with materials being cannibalised for use elsewhere. However, in six new dioceses monastic churches became cathedrals.
- Clearly there was shift in land ownership, particularly among the younger sons of gentry. The number of landowners grew – this was to have significant effects later on.
- The Crown became significantly wealthier, although most of its wealth was spent on paying for the wars.

Spot the inference

High-level answers avoid summarising or paraphrasing the sources, and instead make inferences from the sources. Below is a series of statements. Read Source 1 and decide which of the statements:

- make inference from the source (I)
- paraphrase the source (P)
- summarise the source (S)
- cannot be justified from the source (X).

Statement	I	P	S	X
Richard Ingworth had closed three friaries in Gloucester.				
The mayor and aldermen had already written to Cromwell to tell him this news.				
Black Friars is a proper house as opposed to one that was fictional.				
The Bell family stand to do well out of the closure of the three friaries in Gloucester.				
Ingworth is asking that Master Bell should be allowed to lease the Black Friars House.				
The Grey Friars house is newly built.				
The former friars wish to become priests.				

Doing reliability well

Below are a series of definitions listing reasons why sources can be unreliable. Explain why Source 2 is either reliable or unreliable for the purpose stated, justifying your answer by referring to the following definitions:

- **Vested interest**: the source is written so that the writer can protect their power or their own interests.
- **Second-hand report**: the writer of the source is not an eyewitness, but is relying on someone else's account.
- **Expertise**: the source is written on a subject in which the author (for example a historian) is an expert.
- **Political bias**: the source is written by a politician and it reflects their political views.
- **Reputation**: the source is written to protect the writer's reputation.

This source is reliable/unreliable as evidence of the protests against the Dissolutions of Monasteries throughout the country because

SOURCE 1

(Letter from Richard Ingworth, Commissioner to Thomas Cromwell, 1538)

In Gloucester I have discharged three houses, as by the mayor and alderman's hands you may perceive. The Black Friars, a proper little house, little lead but one aisle, no rents but their gardens, the which Master Bell the alderman hath in lease under their convent seal for many years and I heartily desire you be a good Lord to him that he also may have that house. He doth much good in the town among the poor people, setting many on work, above 300 daily … The Grey Friars is a goodly house, much of it new builded … The White Friars but a small house and in decay. Young Thomas Bell hath part of the garden of it for years. I would he might have that house if it pleased the King's grace and your Lordship. I beseech your Lordship to have discharge for these friars to change their apparel to become secular priests [list of names follows].

SOURCE 2

(From an account of what happened when the commissioners went to Exeter, by John Hooker, a city official, writing during the reign of Elizabeth I)

[The commissioners arrived at the priory of St Nicholas] and commanded a man in the time of their absence to pull down the roof loft in the church. In the meantime, and before they did return, certain women and wives in the city, … minding to stop the suppressing of that house, came in all haste to the said church, some with spikes, some with shovels, some with pikes, and, the church door being fast, broke it open. And, finding there the man pulling down the roof loft, they all sought all the means they could, to take him and hurled stones unto him, in so much that for his safety he was driven to take to the tower for refuge.

Section 4: The Dissolution of the Monasteries

Faction and political infighting in Henry's court

Henry VIII was an absolute monarch who ruled from the court. After the downfall of Wolsey, there was no alternative centre of power. By 1536, he was Head of State and Church. Henry was prepared to listen to advice, and even welcomed debate, but ultimately he made the decisions. His court was torn by factions and infighting. All those who aspired to power and influence needed to be close to him. Everyone was plotting against each other. Any absence from court was not only career threatening, it could be dangerous. Increasingly, Henry was using an **Act of Attainder** to get rid of those who had fallen from favour. No trial was necessary, the word of the King was enough.

Fall of the Boleyn faction

Like Catherine of Aragon, Anne Boleyn had failed to provide Henry with the required male heir. People noticed the disharmony between them, not least because Anne was interfering in religious matters. Meanwhile, Henry fell in love with Jane Seymour. This was excellent news for the Seymour family, whose members were rapidly promoted in the same way that Anne Boleyn's had been.

The Seymours allied with Thomas Cromwell to remove the Boleyns. Cromwell disliked **the Boleyn faction** for various reasons:

- They supported France, when he thought Henry should be pursuing an alliance with Charles V.
- They wanted some of the revenues from the Dissolution of the Monasteries to be spent on the development of the Church and education, instead of enhancing the wealth of the Crown.
- He had felt personally threatened by John Skip's sermon against greed (page 58).

Cromwell accused Anne Boleyn of adultery and witchcraft. Most historians agree that Henry listened to Cromwell because he wanted to get rid of her himself.

- He believed she couldn't give him an heir.
- He believed the accusations of witchcraft, justifying his action in marrying her by saying she had bewitched him.
- He wanted to marry Jane Seymour.
- He was personally affronted by the rumour that Anne had said he was a poor lover – treasonable comments in Henry's court.

Anne was executed in 1536 and her family fell from power. Henry married Jane Seymour, who died in 1537 after the birth of Edward. However, this did not mean Cromwell was secure. By the summer of 1540, ambassadors commented on the tense atmosphere at court. Henry had married Anne of Cleves to cement an alliance brokered by Cromwell with German Protestant princes. Now he wanted both to divorce Anne and end the alliance. Cromwell could facilitate neither.

Fall of Cromwell

On the surface, in June 1540, Cromwell still seemed in favour. Henry had made him Earl of Essex and head of the Privy Chamber; but he could be swayed almost on a whim. The Duke of Norfolk introduced Henry to his niece Catherine Howard, and Henry was besotted. Norfolk felt confident to move against Cromwell in July. He was accused of corruption, and being a heretic. Cromwell was arrested and executed by Act of Attainder. This meant there was no need for a trial – possibly because the evidence against him was at best flimsy.

Spectrum of significance

Below is a list of reasons why Anne Boleyn was arrested and executed. Indicate their relative importance by writing their numbers on the spectrum below and justify your placement, explaining why some factors are more important than others.

1. Henry believed Anne Boleyn couldn't give him the desired heir.
2. Henry believed the accusations of witchcraft.
3. Henry wanted to marry Jane Seymour.
4. Henry was offended by the rumour that Anne Boleyn had said he was a poor lover.
5. Henry didn't like Anne's interfering in religious matters.
6. Henry believed Anne Boleyn might be a heretic.
7. Henry trusted Thomas Cromwell more than Anne Boleyn.
8. Henry had tired of Anne Boleyn.
9. Anne Boleyn nagged Henry.

⟵─────────────────────────⟶

Very important   Less important

You're the examiner (a)

Below are a sample exam-style part (a) question and a paragraph written in answer to this question. Read the paragraph and the mark scheme provided on pages 4–5. Decide which level you would award the paragraph. Write the level below, along with a justification for your choice.

> How far do Sources 1, 2 and 3 suggest that Cromwell fell from power because he was a commoner? Explain your answer using the evidence of Sources 1, 2 and 3.

Source 1 suggests that Cromwell's birth was held against him, for example where it says that he is a man of low birth who held his 'betters' in contempt. Source 3 hints at this too, when Norfolk says traitors do not sit with gentlemen; a lot here depends on his definition of gentlemen, whether he means well-born people or decent people who weren't traitors. Source 1 suggests Cromwell was overthrown because he was a secret Protestant, while Source 2 concentrates on his corruption. However, there is no indication of how significant this actually was in his downfall, whereas Source 1 seems confident on his heresies — and worse, leading others into them. However, we should remember that this is the actual Act of Attainder and may have been used because the evidence might not stand up in court. Norfolk is accusatory but he isn't giving any evidence in support.

Level: Reasons for choosing this level:

SOURCE 1

(From the Parliament roll of 1540, listing the charges made against Thomas Cromwell in the Act of Attainder used to avoid the necessity of a trial)

Thomas Cromwell, contrary to the trust and confidence that your majesty had in him, caused many of your majesty's faithful subjects to be greatly influenced by heresies and other errors, contrary to the right laws and pleasure of Almighty God. And in the last day of March 1539, when certain new preachers such as Robert Barnes were committed to the Tower of London for preaching and teaching against your highness's proclamations, Thomas Cromwell confirmed the preacher to be good. And moreover the said Thomas Cromwell, being a man of very base and low degree, has held the nobles of your realm in great disdain, derision and detestation.

SOURCE 2

(From Robert Hutchinson, Thomas Cromwell, *published 2007)*

There is no doubt he was dipping his venal fingers into the royal money pot as it received the proceeds of the privatisation of the monasteries. His accounts record a number of sales of silver and gold that look suspiciously like spoil from dissolved priories.

SOURCE 3

(From an alleged speech by the Duke of Norfolk, when Cromwell joined the other Privy Councillors on 10 June 1540)

Cromwell! Do not sit there! That is no place for you! Traitors do not sit among gentlemen.

Section 4: The Dissolution of the Monasteries

Henry VIII – authority and religion

The English Reformation

Henry considered himself an absolute monarch who was always right. He was the prime mover in most of the major events originated by the Government. He was, however, human – changeable, sometimes persuaded by the last person he spoke to and often irrational in his belief. In considering the English Reformation therefore, Henry has to be at the heart of the study.

Henry believed he should be head of both Church and State. The question of the divorce was the catalyst. Advisers such as Cranmer provided him with evidence from antiquity. Henry believed that like the Old Testament kings, royal authority came from God and must therefore supersede that of the Church.

The origins of Royal Supremacy

In creating the idea of Royal Supremacy, Henry had certain immoveable ideas:

- He was an active Head of the Church, involved in both religious and political policies.
- Parliament's main role was to rubber-stamp his decisions.
- Henry believed kings, not priests, were religious leaders, so he could appoint religious officials.
- While he would listen to and join debate, he made the decisions. When his mind was made up, his will had to be carried out at the time – even if he changed it later.
- Henry remained conservative in his theology. He would not join an alliance of Protestant princes in 1538 because it would have involved him subscribing to the **Confession of Augsburg**, a statement of Protestant beliefs. He listened to debate and even seemed to support a movement towards Protestantism for example with the Ten Articles of 1536. Ultimately however he imposed his will with the Six Articles of 1539.

Cromwell's Injunctions – ensuring allegiance to the king

Henry believed that both clergy and laity owed the king complete allegiance. In order to insure this, he made Cromwell, a layman, head of the administration of the Church. In his new role Cromwell made injunctions to suppress the monasteries in 1535, to tell bishops how to conduct their affairs in 1536 and to destroy religious relics and discourage pilgrimages, in 1538.

Henry and Protestantism

Henry did not actively seek out heresy. He appeared to welcome moderate debate and didn't challenge even senior Church people on their religious beliefs – although given his belief in divine right, he probably assumed they all agreed with him.

Henry's theology and the Church

Henry remained Catholic in his own beliefs, and the Six Articles were a manifestation of this. He had listened to debate and was now imposing his will. They may have been to reassure Catholics and warn Protestant thinkers from going too far. His major policy statements came in the King's Book of 1543 and 'Golden speech of 1547,' when he attacked both the abuses of Rome and religious reformers.

Henry imagined the future of Christianity as being national churches governed by kings who had the support of their subjects. While accepting debate, he believed those subjects would ultimately agree with the king because he knew best.

Add own knowledge

Below are a sample exam-style part (b) question and the three sources referred to in the question. In one colour, draw links between the sources to show ways in which they agree about the importance of Henry in determining policy. In another colour, draw links between the sources to show ways they disagree. Around the edge of the sources, write relevant own knowledge. Again, draw links to show the ways in which this agrees and disagrees with the sources.

> Do you agree with the view that Henry VIII was the prime mover in the English Reformation in the 1530s? Explain your answer using Sources 1, 2 and 3 and your own knowledge.

SOURCE 1

(From JRH Moorman, A History of the Church in England, 1973)

Henry certainly expected, as Supreme Head, to dictate what a man should believe as well as what he should do. In 1536, he had assisted in the passing by Convocation of the Ten Articles, which were issued by the King with a preface he himself had composed.

SOURCE 2

(From K Randell, Henry VIII and the Reformation in England, 2001)

By 1533, the King had made up his mind – and his determination grew rather than diminished throughout the rest of his life – that he was going to be as much in control of the Church as he was of the rest of his kingdom. Thus, the Royal Supremacy, as it emerged, was to be his (and his alone) of right and was to be effective in practice rather than being the empty title that many of the higher clergy hoped and imagined it would be. Not only in the Act of Supremacy itself was Henry careful to ensure that this was so, but also in all the acts of parliament that followed and in all the authorised statements of policy that were published the message was the same.

SOURCE 3

(Advice to Thomas Cromwell from Sir Thomas More, 1532)

Master Cromwell, if you follow my poor advice, you shall, in your counsel, giving (to) His Grace, ever tell him what he ought to do, but never tell him what he is able to do. So shall you show yourself to be a true and faithful servant, and a right worthy councillor. For if a lion knew his own strength (it would be hard) for any man to rule him.

Recommended reading

Below is a list of further reading on this topic:
- Eamon Duffy, *The Stripping of the Altars*, pp 380–423 (1992).
- Anthony Fletcher, *Tudor Rebellions*, pp 21–48 (second edition 1974).
- Geoffrey Moorhouse, *The Pilgrimage of Grace* (2003).
- Joyce Youngs, *The Dissolution of the Monasteries*, pp 21–117 (1971).

Section 4: The Dissolution of the Monasteries

Section 4: Exam focus

Revised

On pages 69–71 are sample A grade answers to the exam-style questions on these two pages. Read the answers and the examiner comments around them.

a) How far do sources 1, 2 and 3 support the claim that the most significant reason for the Pilgrimage of Grace was the loss of charitable work as a result of Dissolution of the Monasteries? Explain your answer using the evidence of Sources 1, 2 and 3.

b) Do you agree with the view that the main effect of the Dissolution of the Monasteries was to raise revenues for the Crown? Explain your answer using Sources 4, 5 and 6 and your own knowledge.

SOURCE 1

(From the deposition of Robert Aske, leader of the Pilgrimage of Grace in 1536. His statements were taken before his execution in 1537)

The said Aske says that he opposed the suppression of the monasteries because the abbeys in the north gave alms to poor men and laudably served God. And by the suppression, the service of God is greatly diminished. The Church of God is damaged and pulled down, the ornaments and relics of the Church are irreverently treated and tombs of honourable and nobler men pulled down and sold. There is no hospitality now kept in those parts, nor places for travellers to stay, and the profits of the abbeys now go out of the area to the King.

SOURCE 2

(Verses from a ballad composed by the monks of Sawley Abbey at the time of the Pilgrimage of Grace)

Alack! Alack!
For the Church sake
Poor commons wake
And no marvel!
For clear it is
The decay of this
How the poor shall miss
No tongue can tell
For there have had
Both ale and bread
At time of need
And succour great
In all distress
And heaviness
And well intrete [sic]

SOURCE 3

(From a petition of advice to the pilgrims assembled at Pontefract. It was possibly written by Sir Thomas Tempest, an MP who was too ill to attend)

Item, the false flatterer says he will make the richest man in Christendom. But a man can have no more of us than we have, which in manner he has already and yet not satisfied. I think he goes about to make him the poorest Prince in Christendom, for when by such pillage he has lost the hearts of his baronage and poor commons, the riches of the realm are spent and his oath and faith broken, who will then love or trust him?

SOURCE 4

(From G Moorhouse, The Pilgrimage of Grace, *published 2002)*

As it was, the property speculators who might have been stopped in their tracks had the great rebellion have succeeded, made fortunes out of the Dissolution of the Monasteries: men like Alderman Sir Richard Gresham, a Londoner and the purchaser of Fountains Abbey who, in 1539, descended on York, where he bought more than 400 dwellings that had belonged to the city's religious houses, which he then milked for their rents in a cash flow that went down to the capital instead of circulating around York. The draining of northern wealth was one of the complaints that Robert Aske in particular made. On top of that was what the Crown creamed off the Dissolution, which doubled its income at the start of Henry's reign to £200,000 by 1540.

SOURCE 5

(From JRH Moorman, A History of the Church in England, *published 1973)*

So in the course of three years were expunged from the face of England one of the greatest and most ancient of her institutions. It was monks who had evangelised England, whether from Rome or from Iona. It was monks who kept scholarship alive in the Dark Ages, who had established the earliest schools, who had provided hospitality for the traveller, and the pilgrim and nursed the sick. Now by the rapacity of a king and the subservience of Parliament, the whole thing was brought to an end, the monastic lands were transferred to lay owners, and the monastic buildings sank into decay, a useful quarry for farmers who wanted good stone to build their barns and fences.

SOURCE 6

(Extracts from Augmentation Accounts, 1536–38)

Received:

(From land purchase)	£27,732: 2s: 9 1/2d
Received from the sale of gold and silver plate	£6,987: 8s: 11 1/2d
Received from religious houses as fines for exemption from suppression:	
	£5,948: 6s: 8d
Total	£29,847: 16s: 5d

a) How far do sources 1, 2 and 3 support the claim that the most significant reason for the Pilgrimage of Grace was the loss of charitable work as a result of Dissolution of the Monasteries? Explain your answer using the evidence of Sources 1, 2 and 3.

Cross-referencing sources in introduction to address question focus.

Attributes of source.

Using sources in combination to address focus of 'how far.'

Taken together, the three sources show there were various reasons for the Pilgrimage of Grace. Both Sources 1 and 2 do focus on the loss of charitable work as a result of the suppression of the monasteries. Source 3, however, shows there were other reasons, such as the King receiving bad advice from evil councillors, presumably in this instance Cromwell. Aske too goes beyond the issue of the suppression of the monasteries, moving on the desecration of the churches. Sources 1 and 2 emphasise the central role the Church played in people's lives and how the loss would be badly felt.

Aske in Source 1 is talking before his execution. He could therefore be expected to be reliable, that these are genuinely held beliefs because he is dying for them. He talks of the end of hospitality but adds that the work of God is 'greatly diminished'; this ties in with the notion of good works being necessary for salvation. Source 2, on the other hand, is more concerned with the concrete element of charitable works — how will the poor survive? The ballad is written by monks who would have felt threatened, not least because even if their monasteries weren't at that time about to be closed, they may have realised it was possible in the future. Aske talks about the spoliation of churches, and how the profits from the closures go to the King. Source 3 also mentions this; by the dissolution, Cromwell has intended to make Henry rich rather than by implication, the desire to benefit others.

69

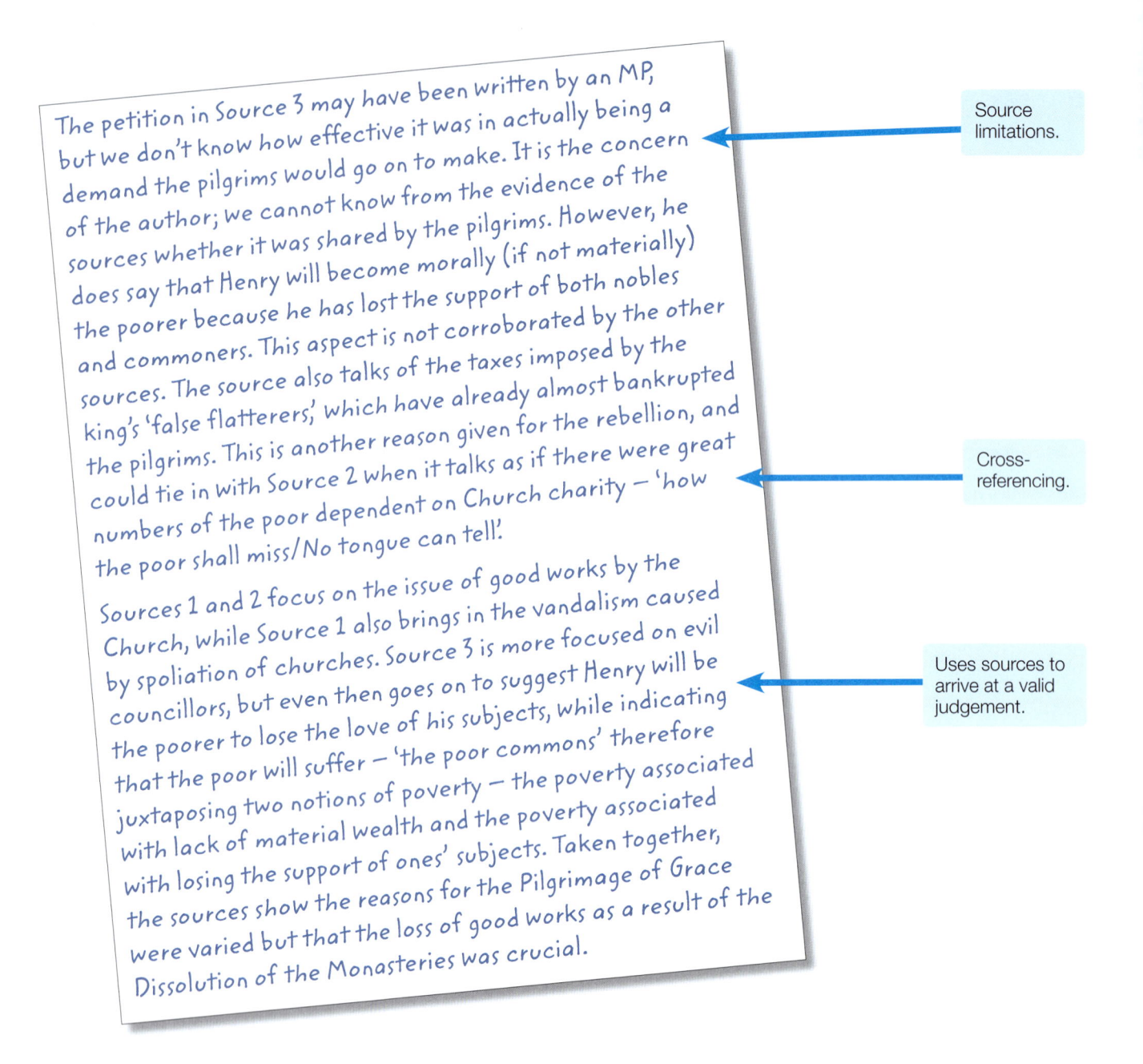

Section 4: The Dissolution of the Monasteries

> The petition in Source 3 may have been written by an MP, but we don't know how effective it was in actually being a demand the pilgrims would go on to make. It is the concern of the author; we cannot know from the evidence of the sources whether it was shared by the pilgrims. However, he does say that Henry will become morally (if not materially) the poorer because he has lost the support of both nobles and commoners. This aspect is not corroborated by the other sources. The source also talks of the taxes imposed by the king's 'false flatterers,' which have already almost bankrupted the pilgrims. This is another reason given for the rebellion, and could tie in with Source 2 when it talks as if there were great numbers of the poor dependent on Church charity – 'how the poor shall miss/ No tongue can tell'.
>
> Sources 1 and 2 focus on the issue of good works by the Church, while Source 1 also brings in the vandalism caused by spoliation of churches. Source 3 is more focused on evil councillors, but even then goes on to suggest Henry will be the poorer to lose the love of his subjects, while indicating that the poor will suffer – 'the poor commons' therefore juxtaposing two notions of poverty – the poverty associated with lack of material wealth and the poverty associated with losing the support of ones' subjects. Taken together, the sources show the reasons for the Pilgrimage of Grace were varied but that the loss of good works as a result of the Dissolution of the Monasteries was crucial.

(Annotations: Source limitations. Cross-referencing. Uses sources to arrive at a valid judgement.)

20/20
The sources are used critically to address the question of 'how far?' Different emphases are recognised. There is some analysis of the language and tone of the sources to address the question.

b) Do you agree with the view that the main effect of the Dissolution of the Monasteries was to raise revenues for the Crown? Explain your answer using Sources 4, 5 and 6 and your own knowledge.

Using sources to address the question focus.

Both Sources 4 and 6 show how wealthy the Crown had become by the Dissolution of the Monasteries. This was a significant reason for their suppression. However, there were other effects. Source 5 for example considers the loss of the monasteries with their cultural history and good works. Source 4 also shows how individuals could gain from the sale of their lands and properties. Indeed, people were enquiring about land purchases before legislation to enable the actual dissolution process to take place had been completed.

Sets question parameters.

In this essay, using the sources and other knowledge we will examine how significant the growth of government revenue was as an effect of the dissolution in comparison with others, such as the loss of the monasteries.

Challenging source's usefulness in terms of question focus.

On the surface, Source 6 shows some impressive accounting — a total of £29,847 16s and 5d received from the sale of property and plate over a three-year period. However, the figures are incomplete; they don't include expenses incurred and don't tell us what the Crown did with this revenue. If the Crown was bankrupt, for example, at the start, such revenues would not make it rich, but simply go towards paying off debts already occurred, such as the cost of subsidising Henry's European allies. While Source 4 shows that the Crown received huge sums, it also indicates that individuals did very well out of the dissolution.

Source supported by accurate factual material.

Having said this, Henry didn't give the land away. Henry only gave 69 out of 1,593 land grants as gifts. The Church lands were sold off at market values, but inevitably proved a good investment.

Integrates sources with knowledge to move the answer on.

Source 4 shows how Gresham, a London merchant, could buy lots of former Church property in York. It also suggests that the revenues flowed south to London. This was something Aske had complained about. People in the north of England felt remote from government. The King rarely, if ever, visited his northern counties, and there was sense that central government had little idea of their culture and values. Certainly, many more opposed the religious changes in the North than the South.

Challenges representation made in source.

Some historians make great play about the loss of Church culture. Source 5 talks sadly about the loss of monastic culture and mentions all the ways in which monks had contributed to our culture. However, there is evidence that monastic life

71

Section 4: The Dissolution of the Monasteries

was already in decline before the dissolutions. The author does mention the destruction of monastic buildings, which many have decried — referring often to licensed vandalism in the spoliations. However, as the source acknowledges the materials were recycled to build barns and so on, and there is also evidence that the fortifications Henry was building in the event of French invasion in 1539 came from former monastic buildings. Not all monasteries were destroyed, however — some were converted to great houses, and some monastic churches became cathedrals. Henry created six new dioceses in Lichfield and Bristol, for example, and their cathedrals were formerly monastic churches. Source 4 mentions that Gresham bought Fountains Abbey, but it doesn't indicate that he left it to decay in the way the author of Source 5 suggests new owners did.

Uses knowledge to challenge information from the source.

He does, however, lament the demise of the monks. Other historians such as John Guy have written that the standards of the clergy declined as a result of the dissolution. The Church no longer offered such a prestigious profession, and suffered some decline in morale. There were fewer clergy in the House of Lords as a result of the dissolutions, and therefore their influence in government fell. Also it should go without saying that the risk of the monasteries being hostile to government policy disappeared.

Discriminating use of evidence to come to a valid judgement.

It can be seen from the evidence of the sources that the effects of the dissolutions were diverse and varied. However, a major motive had been the desire for the Crown to grow rich from the sales and at least in the short term, this is what seemed to happen. It should not be forgotten, however, that other people grew rich too. Source 4 mentions both the Crown and individuals, while Source 6 gives an admittedly incomplete account of the revenues raised. The loss of the culture accruing from the closure of the monasteries would probably not have been a big factor in Henry's thinking when he and Cromwell decided to dissolve the monasteries and take their wealth for the Crown.

40/40
This essay is tightly argued, using knowledge to both challenge and develop the information contained in the sources to address the question, whose focus is never lost. A well-balanced judgement brings the answer together.

What makes a good answer?

You have now considered eight sample A-grade essays throughout the course of this revision guide. Use these essays to make a bullet-pointed list of the characteristics of an A-grade essay. Use this list when planning and writing your own practice exam essays.

Timeline

1509	Henry VIII inherits the throne
	Henry VIII marries Catherine of Aragon
	Thomas Wolsey appointed Royal Almoner
1511–14	Richard Hunne case
1512	Westminster Palace burnt down
1511–12	First French War
1513	War against the French and Scots
1514	Wolsey made Archbishop of York
	Death of Louis XII of France; succeeded by Francis I
1515	Wolsey made Cardinal (November) and Lord Chancellor (December)
1516	Death of King Ferdinand of Spain; succeeded by Charles V
	Birth of Princess Mary
1517	Sweating sickness epidemic
1518	Wolsey made Papal legate
	Treaty of London
1519	Death of Holy Roman Emperor Maximilian; succeeded by Charles V
	Affair of the Minions
1520	Meeting between Henry VIII and Francis I at the Field of the Cloth of Gold
1521	Henry VIII given title Defender of the Faith
	Secret treaty between Henry VIII and Charles V against France
1523	Rebellion against Francis I led by the Duc de Bourbon
1524–29	Wolsey closed 29 monasteries
1525	Amicable Grant
	Battle of Pavia – Francis I taken prisoner
1526	Eltham Ordinances
1527	Henry's desire for an annulment
	Imperial troops sack Rome
1528	Cardinal Campeggio arrived to join with Wolsey in judging the validity of Henry's marriage
	Legatine court opens
1529	Battle of Landriano – French defeated in Italy
	Fall of Wolsey
	Meeting of 'Reformation Parliament'
1530	Hampton Court Conference
	Death of Wolsey en route to hear treason charges against him
1531	Henry accuses all clergy of praemunire and fines them £100,000
1532	Meeting between Henry VIII and Francis I at Calais
	Henry judged Papal dispensation for his marriage to Catherine of Aragon invalid
1532–34	Seven Acts to create the English Church headed by Henry VIII:
	■ Conditional Restraint of Annates
	■ Act in Restraint of Annates
	■ Act for Submission of the Clergy
	■ Ecclesiastical Appointments Act
	■ Act Forbidding Papal Dispensations and payment of Peter's Pence
	■ Act of Supremacy
	■ Succession and Treason Act
1533	Marriage of Henry VIII and Anne Boleyn
	Birth of Elizabeth
	Pope Clement VII decides Henry's marriage to Catherine is legal
1534	Death of Pope Clement VII; succeeded by Paul III
1535	Henry VIII excommunicated
	Executions of Sir Thomas More and Bishop Fisher for refusing to accept the oath of Surpremacy
	Visitations to Monasteries and Valor Ecclesiaticus
1536	Rebellions in Lincolnshire, Yorkshire and the north-west – the Pilgrimage of Grace
	Death of Catherine of Aragon
	Dissolution of Smaller Monasteries Act
	Execution of Anne Boleyn; downfall of her supporters
	Marriage of Henry VIII to Jane Seymour
	Act of the Ten Articles
1537	Birth of Edward, male heir
	Death of Jane Seymour
	Bishops' Book
1538–40	Closure of larger monasteries
1538	Actions against relics, shrines etc
1539	Second Dissolution Act
	Act of the Six Articles
1540	Marriage of Henry to Anne of Cleves
	Fall of Thomas Cromwell

Glossary

Act of Attainder An Act passed through Parliament that declared the accused guilty with no need for a trial.

Aquitaine Area of South-western France governed by England from 1154 until lost during the Hundred Years War in 1453.

Boleyn faction A group of courtiers who associated themselves with Anne Boleyn and her family, who worked to help Henry VIII obtain his divorce and have Anne crowned Queen.

Collective security States agreeing to protect each other from any foreign aggression.

Comperta The findings of the 1535 Visitations.

Confession of Augsburg statement of Protestant beliefs drawn up by Protestant princes.

Consummated Refers to the first time a couple have sex after getting married which confirms the legitimacy of the marriage.

Court of Augmentations Court set up to deal with the sale of land following the Dissolution of the monasteries.

Court of the Star Chamber Court of law made up of Privy Councillors and judges.

Crown An English coin introduced as part of Henry VIII's monetary reform of 1526 with the value of five shillings.

Eltham Ordinances Wolsey's attempt to reform the king's household in 1525.

Excommunicated Expelled from the Roman Catholic Church.

Extra parliamentary grant Grant imposed without the consent of Parliament.

Henrican Church The name given to the Church created after the break with Rome.

Holy Roman Empire Empire based in central Europe and Germany.

Imperial ideas Desire for conquest.

King's Council Body of advisors who helped the king govern.

Legatine Court Court set up under Cardinals Wolsey and Campeggio to examine the validity of Henry VIII's marriage to Catherine of Aragon.

Livre The currency of France until 1795.

Lord Chancellor The most important minister of the king.

Lord Privy Seal Important minister who kept the seals used to authenticate royal orders.

Lutheran Religious ideas associated with Martin Luther, particularly 'Justification by Faith', meaning that belief in the teachings of Jesus alone was enough for personal salvation.

Mustered levies People called up to act as a sort of home guard against possible invasion.

Nemesis Person responsible for someone's downfall.

Ninety-five theses Martin Luther's attack on the abuses in the Roman Catholic Church.

Papal bull Policy decision from the Pope.

Papal legate or **Legate a latere** Most powerful churchman with extensive powers over the Church in England.

Peter's Pence Tax collected for the Pope.

Pilgrimage of Grace Name given to the rebellion in the North of England in 1536.

Pluralcies Where priests had more than one living.

Pontefract Articles Statement about the aims of the Pilgrimage of Grace drawn up at Pontefract in Yorkshire.

Praemunire Obscure fourteenth-century law preventing Papal law from overriding that of England.

Purgatory Catholic belief that the soul stays in limbo until people have been purged of their sins and can enter heaven.

Reformation Name given to the break with Papal control of the English Church (elsewhere in Europe, also refers to the break with the Roman Catholic Church).

Renaissance Name given to the flowering of knowledge in the late fifteenth to early seventeenth centuries, focusing particularly on science, art, and the rediscovery of the ancient world.

Royal Almoner Office responsible for distributing alms to the poor.

Royal progress Where the court moved around its various palaces usually during the summer months.

Royal Supremacy When Henry made himself Head of the Church in England.

Schmalkaldic League Alliance of Protestant princes in Germany, formed in 1531.

Sufficiently Abundant Collections Collection of old documents Henry used to justify his break with Rome and make himself Supreme Head of the Church in England.

Supplication against the Ordinaries Petition by Parliament in 1532 against bishops abusing their position.

Thomas Becket Much venerated saint, murdered on the orders of King Henry II in 1170.

Answers

Section 1: Henry VIII and the quest for international influence

Page 7, Support or challenge?

Only Source 1 supports the statement. It states that the Holy League was formed to expel the French from Italy. However, Sources 2 and 3 suggest that Henry and Ferdinand had their own separate agendas for going to war – Henry to capture Aquitaine and Ferdinand to capture Navarre.

Page 7, Spot the mistake

The sources are simply used for the information they offer. There is no attempt to integrate the sources or to explain 'How far …?'.

Page 9, Highlighting integration

The second response is at a higher level because it integrates the sources, comparing them – for example by showing how the third source agrees with the first.

Page 13, Write the question: suggested answer

Valid exam questions would be on the lines of:

How far do the sources agree that Henry was seen as a peacemaker in Europe?

Or

'How far do Sources 1, 2 and 3 suggest that the Pope expected Henry's help in his conflict with Charles V?'

Page 17, Eliminate irrelevance

Henry's main reason for seeking a Protestant alliance was his continuing fear of French invasion. Sources 1 and 2 both show that the invasion threat was real and Henry needed powerful friends. The first source shows that Henry was vulnerable to attack because he had been excommunicated and France and Spain were now friends. Source 2 goes further, suggesting that Catholic superpowers are preparing to invade England. ~~Cromwell was singled out in particular as a bad influence. The Pope didn't like him because he had organised the reformation and dissolution of the monasteries.~~ The fear of invasion by France was growing because France controlled the entire European coastline opposite southern England and was building a large navy at its shipyards in Brest and Havre de Grave. Henry's marriage to Anne of Cleves, whose brother was an important German prince, helped cement Henry's Protestant alliance. Henry hoped that France would not invade England if Germany would come to his aid. ~~However, he didn't find Anne of Cleves very attractive and tried to get out of the marriage. Anne was unsophisticated and a bit dumpy. Her German clothes didn't flatter her. But he couldn't just end the relationship her for fear of upsetting her brother.~~

Section 2: Structure of government

Page 25, Support or challenge?

Source 1 challenges the statement in the question in two ways. First, it suggests that Henry chose Wolsey because Wolsey was willing to follow Henry's lead. It also suggests that he chose Wolsey because they worked very well together. Source 2 also challenges the statement because it shows Wolsey's other qualities such as his political vision and because he had wider goals beyond personal motives. Source 3, on the other hand, clearly supports the statement because it points to Wolsey's ability to see clear and cohesive ways of achieving Henry's goals.

Page 27, Identify an argument

Sample 2 contains the argument.

Page 31, Write the question: suggested answer

Valid exam questions would be on the lines of:

Use Sources 1, 2 and 3 and your own knowledge.

Do you agree that Thomas Wolsey dominated government in the years up until 1529? Explain your answer using the evidence of Sources 1, 2 and 3 and your own knowledge.

Or

Use Sources 1, 2 and 3 and your own knowledge.

'Ministers needed personal relationships with Henry VIII in order to govern effectively.' Do you agree with this statement?

Explain your answer using the evidence of Sources 1, 2 and 3 and your own knowledge.

Page 33, Doing reliability well: suggested answer

Source 1 is unreliable in the sense that it reflects the vested interests of the author who clearly would not wish to highlight any opposition to the taxes and for the same reason it reflects his political bias. Source 2 is unreliable in the sense that it reflects the Duke of Norfolk's vested interest. He is responsible for upholding the law and therefore assures the King that the protestors couldn't pay rather than wouldn't pay, and they remained loyal to the King. However, if his intention is assurance, his report may not be accurate about the level of, or causes of resentment.

Source 3 is reliable in that the historian is using his expertise to imply the extent of the resistance through the use of examples; although it doesn't indicate how effective this resistance was or what action was taken.

Page 35, Develop the detail: suggested answer

Sources 1 and 2 imply that it was not the King who was Wolsey's main enemy. **Source 1 argues that Henry was neither Wolsey's 'fiercest enemy' nor was he seeking his 'complete bloody destruction.' Indeed, Source 2 indicates that Wolsey had 'become a habit', suggesting that the king had an emotional need for his minister**. However, both sources agree that Wolsey had other powerful enemies who were seeking his destruction. **Source 1 simply notes that 'if Henry had momentarily faltered, Wolsey's enemies were quick to push the king onwards.' But Source 1 does not say explicitly who these enemies were**. Wolsey had many enemies, including members of the nobility who envied his power, and taxpayers, who resented the taxes he imposed. Source 2 comes close to specifically identifying the Boleyn faction as being responsible. **It states that 'another had interposed herself' referring to Anne Boleyn, who replaced Wolsey as the King's confidante. Furthermore, it was only after 1529, when Wolsey lost the support of the Boleyn faction, that his position weakened**. In this sense, Henry's opposition was not the most important factor in the dismissal of Wolsey because the plotting of the Boleyn faction prompted Henry to dismiss a minister he had once trusted.

Page 35, Spot the inference

Henry relied on others for advice and support. (S)

Anne Boleyn's relatives realised they could use her influence with the King to bring about the fall of Wolsey. (I)

Wolsey was a habit that was difficult to break. (S)

Anne Boleyn could influence the King in his political decision making. (X)

Henry didn't rely on Anne Boleyn for political advice but her relatives realised they could use her as a bridgehead to influence him. (P)

Section 3: Henry's changing relations with the Catholic Church

Page 41, Spot the mistake

The candidate is simply paraphrasing the sources and not answering the question.

Page 43, Spot the inference

Catherine believed she would have a fairer hearing in Rome because the judges would not be unduly influenced by the King. (I)

Catherine believed if the case was heard in Rome, she would win and the divorce would not be granted. (X)

If the case was heard in England, the judges would bend to the King's will. (S)

Catherine wanted the case to be heard in Rome. She could not expect a fair trial from English judges. (P)

Catherine hated Thomas Wolsey. (X)

Page 45, Identify an argument

Sample 1 contains the argument.

Page 47, Develop the detail: suggested answer

Sources 1 and 3 agree that Thomas Cromwell's role was very significant. Source 1 says what an achievement the Reformation was and it was largely down to him – '**he did great things that amaze one who has considered them well'**. Source 3 agrees, talking about his energy and vision. The source goes on to say that he drew up much of the legislation that changed the status of the Church. Source 2 on the other hand suggests he wasn't really responsible; the King was in control all the time **of who served him as ministers and Cromwell might even be dismissed. It suggests moreover that powerful rivals such as the Bishop of Winchester don't like him. There is a suggestion that the King will promote those he had previously rejected and get rid of those like Cromwell whom he had previously promoted. This suggests the King, not Cromwell, was in control of events thereby disagreeing with Sources 1 and 2 about Cromwell's importance.**

Page 49, Eliminate irrelevance

Henry VIII was prepared to go to great lengths to enforce his Protestant Reformation. This suggests that he was fully committed to the Protestant cause. For example, Source 1 refers to 'the martyrdom of priests', a reference to Henry's willingness to execute those who remained committed to the old ways.

These priests included Bishop John Fisher, who, with Sir Thomas More, was executed in 1535 for refusing to accept the Oath of Supremacy. ~~One popular method of execution was burning at the stake. Some, such as Cranmer avoided death by keeping their theology secret.~~ Additionally, Source 2 refers to Henry throwing 'off the Pope's yoke', an anti-Catholic move which indicated that Henry was committed to Protestantism. This move was represented in a mock battle on the Thames in which the barge representing the Pope was sunk by the King's barge. ~~Source 2 also says that 'the reformers offered him in their turn all the flatteries they could decently give' suggesting that they too were committed to bringing about religious change.~~ In this sense, it is clear that there is evidence to support the view that Henry was genuinely committed to a Protestant Reformation in England.

Page 51, You're the examiner

This answer tends to describe what the sources tell us rather than engaging with them critically. It includes some knowledge, which is not required in part (a). It would be marked in the lower part of level 3 because it comprehends the sources, with some attempt at comparison.

Section 4: The Dissolution of the Monasteries

Page 57, Spot the inference

Smaller monasteries were being particularly singled out as being sinful places. (I)

Smaller monasteries were being picked on because they were easier to close. (X)

Smaller monasteries were sinful places where the property was wasted. (S)

All monks and nuns in smaller religious houses lived dissolute lives. (X)

Open sin and disgusting living were daily occurrences in smaller monasteries. (P)

Page 57, Write the question: suggested answer

Typical questions would be along the lines of:

How far do Sources 1, 2 and 3 agree that there was widespread evidence of immorality in the monastic houses in the 1530s?

Explain your answer using the evidence of Sources 1, 2 and 3.

Page 59, Eliminate irrelevance

Sources 1, 2 and 3 all agree that the Dissolution of the Monasteries was essentially a land grab. Cromwell had promised to make Henry as rich as Croesus. ~~Croesus was a fabulously rich king in Greek mythology, who was defeated by the Persians in the Fifth Century BC.~~ Source 1 is an example of the instructions given to the Commissioners to enquire as to the wealth of monasteries, while Source 2 is an example of what they found. ~~Its a pity~~ they're not about the same place, but they do show how rich Henry could become if he was going to acquire all the wealth from the monasteries. Source 3 suggests he would be £100,000 a year better off. ~~That may not seem that much to us when he has a country to run, but prices were much lower in those days so it would be millions and millions in today's values.~~ In this way the sources clearly indicate that the Dissolution of the Monasteries was a land grab because they all stress the wealth that the dissolution will bring to the King.

Page 61, Explain the difference: suggested answer

Clearly there are significant differences in interpretation because one is written by Aske to emphasise the loyalty of the rebels, and the other by the King determined to treat them as traitors.

Page 63, Spot the inference

Richard Ingworth had closed three friaries in Gloucester. (P)

The mayor and aldermen had already written to Cromwell to tell him this news. (P)

Black Friars is a proper house as opposed to one that was fictional. (X)

The Bell family stand to do well out of the closure of the three friaries in Gloucester. (I)

Ingworth is asking that Master Bell should be allowed to lease the Black Friars House. (S)

The Grey Friars house is newly built. (S)

The former friars wish to become priests. (S)

Page 63, Doing reliability well: suggested answer

The source is unreliable as the author was writing many years after the dissolution in Exeter so may have forgotten some of the details. Therefore he is relying on second-hand reports.

Page 65, You're the examiner

The sources are cross-referenced and engaged with critically. Elements of challenge and corroboration are analysed. This answer would be graded at mid-Level 4.

Notes